SEE!

Clear Vision and Good Looks For Life

By William N. May, M.D.

Dear Katy,
It's a pleasure
to care for good friends

13-10 h

Outskirts Press, Inc.
Denver, Colorado

Outskirts Press, Inc.
http://www.outskirtspress.com

ISBN: 978-1-4327-3375-9

Library of Congress Control Number: 2008938443

Outskirts Press and the "OP" logo are trademarks belonging to Outskirts Press, Inc.

PRINTED IN THE UNITED STATES OF AMERICA

Dedication

Everything I do is dedicated to my family, friends, and teachers. This book is specifically dedicated to Marty Head. She inspired its creation on the slopes of Vail. Thank you, Marty, for being such a wonderful person. You made my already full life richer.

Table of Contents

Foreword

When I first finished my training in ophthalmology, I was proud to be able to answer seemingly simple questions in great depth. I eventually noticed that my patients would get this glazed, faraway look as they politely waited for me to finish my lectures. Then, embarrassed that they had not understood a word I said, the visit would be quickly over. I would have an uneasy feeling that I had left them more frightened and confused than before I started the explanation.

After about twenty years as an ophthalmologist, my discussions have evolved into a more basic yet useful form. This book is a collection of what I say on a daily basis to people with confusing and difficult problems.

This book is not meant as an authoritative medical text. It is not meant as a source for scientific or medical information. It is just a collection of discussions I commonly have with my patients. This is an effort to promote dialogue between doctors and patients.

The visual system and its diseases are very complex. So if you wonder what your eye doctor is talking about, this book is a good start. It is meant to provide enough background information to understand the basics of some common eye problems. Then you can better discuss these problems with your ophthalmologist.

There is no substitute for an evaluation by an ophthalmologist. This book is not meant as help with self-diagnosis. That is a dangerous approach to any medical problem. Even I can't check my own eyes! So this book is not designed to help you figure out what is wrong by yourself. After your ophthalmologist tells you what is wrong, you can use information from this book to be actively involved in the prevention and treatment of specific common eye problems.

Chapter 1

How You See

The eye is like a camera, and the front of the eye is like a lens system. The back of the eye is like film. The eye has two lenses. The cornea in the very front of the eye is a rigid lens that doesn't change. It does about two-thirds of the focusing of the light that comes into the eye. There is a second lens just behind the iris (the colored part of the eye). It does about one-third of the focusing.

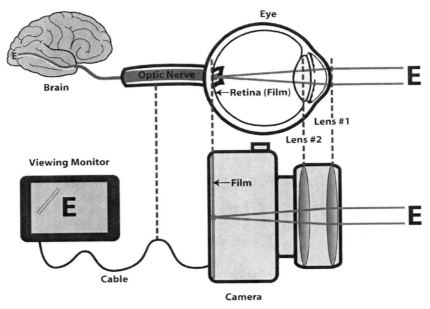

Camera - Brain Analogy

The eye is like a video camera with a view screen. The front is like the adjustable lens system of a video camera on autofocus. When something comes close, the camera automatically adjusts its focus to see near. Then the film on the video camera creates an image which is then sent back to the brain through a cable. The transmission through this cable carries the image all the way to the video monitor at the back of the brain.

One of the many amazing things about the eye is that it has autofocus! When a normal eye looks off into the distance, the two lenses work together to focus light perfectly. However, when things come closer than 20 feet, the eye needs more power to keep its target in focus. This is when the "autofocus" kicks in. The brain notices that an image is coming closer and sends a message to the eye to increase its focusing power. In response to that, a muscle inside the eye contracts. This muscle (the ciliary muscle) changes the shape of the second lens inside the eye. This new shape increases the focusing power of the second lens just enough to keep the target in perfect focus. The brain and the eye do this together without any learning involved.

Ciliary Muscle Actions

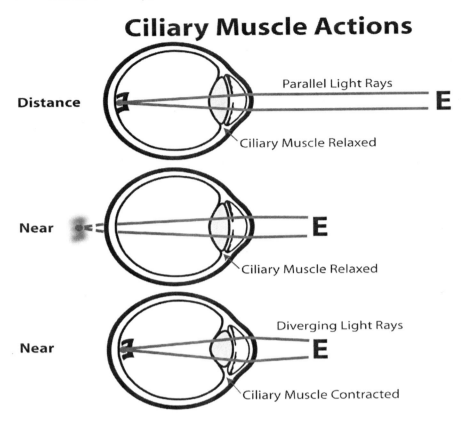

When a normal eye sees an image far away, the light rays coming from that image are parallel (exactly side by side). When the light rays hit the eye, they are bent (focused) a certain amount. If the object we are looking at comes closer, the light rays coming from it spread out. If the front of the eye doesn't change the amount of light bending (focusing power), the object seems blurred when it comes close. The eye automatically increases its ability to bend light (focus) by changing the shape of the lens with the ciliary muscle. With the help of ciliary muscle contraction, the lens gets thicker so it can bend the light (focus) more. Increased light bending brings even light rays spreading out from a near object into focus.

The eye also has an automatic brightness control. Between the two lenses is a hole that opens and closes according to how much light is coming into the eye. This opening is called the pupil. On a very bright day, too much light may come into the eye. In this case the hole in the middle of the eye (the pupil) gets smaller. This is another reaction controlled by the brain. It senses the increased light and sends a signal to close the opening into the eye so that extra light can be stopped from entering. At night when there is very little light, the brain senses the dimness and opens the pupil to allow as much light into the eye as possible.

After light passes through the hole in the colored part of the eye (the pupil), it passes through the internal lens and comes to what doctors call the vitreous gel. This gel fills the middle of the eye. Usually the light passes through this clear part of the eye unobstructed so it can hit the retina.

The retina is another amazing part of the eye. It is like film in a camera. It takes the light focused by the front of the eye and converts it to a signal that can be understood by the brain. To me, this is a stunning concept. Light exists as part of the universe. It is like gravity, a basic part of reality. To be able to take light into the body and interpret colors and images is amazing! Try closing your eyes to see the impact of the loss of this essential human ability.

The retina sends this information to the brain through the optic nerve. When it gets to the brain, it follows a pathway to the part of the brain that puts information together. This optic nerve and the pathways inside the brain are like a cable on a video camera. It passes the information from the camera of the eye to the viewing screen of the brain.

So the eye is more like a video camera. It takes a focused image and transmits it to a viewing screen through a cable. This transmission passes through the whole head to the very back of the brain. This area of the brain is called the occipital cortex. It takes the information from the eye and creates an image. This is like a TV screen.

Chapter 2

Myths

What your mother told you that *is* true: DON'T LOOK AT THE SUN (except at sunset).

Looking at the sun causes an untreatable form of permanent blindness. It usually happens in times of solar eclipse or during episodes of drug use.

Drug-abuse-related blindness usually happens in teenagers.

When you are high and you look at the sun, it doesn't hurt. Apparently the colors are awesome! It must be fascinating to watch the colors while the back of your eye is being burned away. This usually happens in just one eye. "How strange," you might say. "Why would this be?" We ophthalmologists think the answer is that these teenagers remember their mothers warning them not to look into the sun. Even though they are under the influence of drugs, they still remember their mother's warnings. They close one eye just in case she was right. Luckily, this saves the vision in one of their eyes.

The worst cases are the ones who don't remember or don't know about the harmful effects of looking at the sun. Or they may be so high they don't remember what mom said and keep both eyes open. Then both eyes become permanently blind. How tragic! These poor teenagers will never be able to see more detail than the big E on the eye chart. They will need some kind of visual aid to read anything. Their performance in school will be severely impaired. They will have lots of social problems living in the current American teenage world of cell phones, caller ID, Sidekicks®, Blackberrys®, laptops with wireless Internet access, and instant messaging. Television will never seem clear.

This all happens because of a one-time adolescent error in judgment. They stare at the sun for just a few minutes, and the magnifying lenses in the front of the eye bring the sunlight into focus so intensely that holes are burned into the back of their eyes. These burns happen in the part of the eye that sees detail vision. This part of the eye is permanently destroyed.

Solar Eclipse Blindness

Blindness in the U.S. from solar eclipses is rare. The news media usually warns the public quite effectively. There are ways to view the eclipse without blinding yourself, including the use of reflections and cameras.

Advice Related to Looking at the Sun

Don't do it! Don't get so high you can't remember what your mother told you about looking into the sun.

Sitting Too Close to the Television

The light rays coming from modern televisions are not harmful to the eye. They may seem bright. Brightness can cause pain in people who are sensitive to lots of light. This is not really a problem, because these people are probably not sitting right next to the television screen with the brightness turned all the way up. Permanent damage from television light just doesn't happen.

The source of this myth may be that children who sit close

to the TV later need glasses. This does happen. But the need for glasses is not caused by the television. These children are already nearsighted. They can't see the screen from across the room. They have to sit close in order to see. They are too young to know this is not normal.

More advice: If you have children and you keep telling them not to sit so close to the TV, have their eyes tested. They are probably nearsighted.

Reading in the dark: It's okay . . . really.

In World War II, the Japanese Navy did not have radar. Instead, they had people looking out at the dark ocean who were completely adapted to dim light. These lookouts would spend hours in a completely dark room with their eyes open, adjusting to the dark before going on duty. Historians claim they performed extremely well seeing enemy ships.

This makes sense from a scientific point of view. If there is no fog, the healthy human eye can see amazingly well at night. Even under just starlight, a fully dark adjusted human visual system can see a lot. The point is that we are designed to see in the dark. If we read at night in dim lights, this is just what the eyes should do at night. If you have a child who loves to read, even in the dark, that's a good thing! Enjoy having a child who's engaged. If you have a spouse who reads in the dark and keeps doing that even when you tell him not to, give him a break. Maybe he's one of those people who are hurt by bright lights. Relax! They are not hurting themselves. If they like to read in the dark, let them.

Using the Computer Too Much

It is amazing how often people come into my office confessing that their vision is bad because they are using the computer too much. This is like looking at the TV too much. It is just a screen. There is no temporary or permanent damage coming from this level of light. Yes, if you concentrate really hard, you blink less. That causes your eyes to get dry. Then you may have blurred vision, tearing, and eye pain. This causes no permanent damage to the eye. If you hold your eyes open without blinking, you cause the same effect. Yes, you will see less, your eyes will hurt, and they may cry, but there is no permanent damage. As soon as you start blinking, you will be back to normal.

Reading Too Much

For some reason, people think that using their eyes too much hurts them. I think this comes from the problems we all have when we use our muscles too much. Yes, that causes problems. When I play tennis for hours, I get sore. At my old age of 52, if I played tennis for ten hours every day, I might develop real problems.

The eye doesn't work this way. It is like the brain; it never really shuts down. You can use it as much as you want to. It is working all the time anyway. If you close your eyes and concentrate on what you are seeing, you will see a lot! It's really amazing what the eye sends to the brain when the eyes are closed. Try it. Close your eyes and watch. When you sleep, the brain suppresses the input from the eyes, but they are still working. That is why you see all that stuff with your eyes closed.

Using Drugstore Readers, or "Cheaters"

Go ahead and use them. Don't worry. Yes, the lenses in the glasses are the same on both sides. If your eyes are different, they will not be in focus at the same place. So just use one eye to read. It won't hurt anything if you do this. Yes, these lenses will not be centered on your eyes, and that could cause headaches from your brain constantly trying to bring together images separated by these glasses. So what? If you get a headache, just stop using these glasses. Your headache will go away. You will have no permanent damage.

Cheap Sunglasses

Get as many as you want. There was a study done comparing expensive sunglasses to cheap sunglasses as far as the blocking of ultraviolet rays goes. There was no difference! Lots of the cheap ones blocked ultraviolet light better than the expensive ones. This is the only issue from a medical point of view. Yes, the expensive sunglasses might give you a more uniform tint. Yes, these more expensive lenses may give you a little better visual quality. They are certainly more stylish. As far as the health of your eyes goes, reducing the total amount of light and the amount of UV rays matters. Nothing else is important.

Straining Your Eyes

To me, this means trying really hard to see. That could mean trying to force your eyes to see what they cannot see. This may involve a focusing effort by the eyes when they just cannot see, or it may involve not blinking while you try to see what you can't see. Both efforts may cause pain. There is no permanent damage from these efforts. Just stop trying, and you will be fine. Go to your local eye doctor and get glasses! Then you won't have to do this.

Using Just One Eye

Go ahead! This is exactly what millions of people do when they are in "monovision." This means using one eye for near and the other for distance. Using one eye to see near or far hurts nothing. I do it, and it's fine. It causes no damage.

If you cross them, they will get stuck.

No, no, no, this doesn't happen. Some children develop a serious problem related to crossed eyes. This problem can cause permanent decreased vision in one eye. It is not caused by purposefully crossing their eyes. That has nothing to do with it. It is a development problem. If your child's eyes cross, take him to a pediatric ophthalmologist. This is a serious problem that has nothing to do with misbehavior.

Rubbing Your Eyes: the Good, the Bad, and the Ugly

The Good: It feels good.

The Bad: It increases redness and eyelid swelling. If you have an allergic reaction, it gets worse. It may cause bruising on the eye and under the eyelid. Rubbing the eye within a week of LASIK really messes up this surgery.

The Ugly: It promotes permanent bags and wrinkles. It causes temporary swelling.

The amazing thing about the visual system is that it's very resistant to self-imposed injury. Don't worry much about whatever you do with your eyes. Just don't look at the sun, and follow your eye doctor's directions if you have eye surgery.

Chapter 3

Macular Degeneration

To understand macular degeneration, we should first discuss the parts of the eye. Once again, the eye is like a camera. The front is like a lens. The back is like film. The back of the eye is called the retina. It takes the focused light and turns it into a picture.

However, there is a difference between camera film and the retina. All detail vision in the retina comes from a tiny area in the middle that is about the size of the head of a small nail. It is called the macula. When this tiny area is damaged, there can be a significant loss of vision.

Degeneration means a progressive loss of function with a corresponding deterioration of structure. That means important parts of the retina change so that they don't work anymore.

Rods and cones are the receptor cells of the retina. When they are hit by light, they create a message that can be understood by the brain. Without them, there is no vision. They are a rare type of cell because they are not replaced. These permanent cells are made before birth. The same exact cell lives in the same place throughout an individual's life. This is quite different from most cells in the body. Most organs, like the liver, are made up of cells that are constantly dividing to create new cells. The new cells live for a limited time and are then replaced. So, there is a constant birth, growth, and death of cells in most organs.

In the eye, however, the rods and cones do not divide to regenerate themselves. Each cell must remain healthy to be functional throughout life. When cells are permanent, they usually require other cells to repair and rebuild them. If these support cells are lost, the permanent cells degenerate. The loss of support cells and support structures is part of macular degeneration. This causes the loss of the permanent cells that make vision.

Overall Structure of the Eye and Its Function

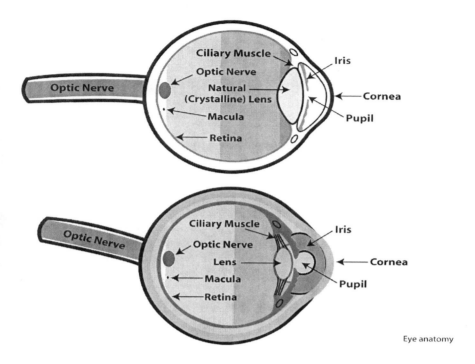

Eye anatomy

The cornea and the lens focus light onto the back of the eye. The iris, by opening and closing the pupil, adjusts the amount of light coming into the eye. Focusing by the front of the eye brings light into focus in one tiny part of the retina called the macula. This is where all detail vision starts.

In age-related macular degeneration (AMD), support cells for the retina are lost. As a result, rods and cones are not repaired, so when they are damaged by light or inflammation, they cannot recover. Because these receptor cells are necessary for detail vision, when they are lost, detail vision is reduced.

When all the central support cells go, eventually all detail vision is lost.

You might wonder what is causing damage to these cells. We do not know the whole story. However, we do know that irritation from light is involved. New studies suggest a hereditary problem with the immune system. This system normally protects against infection. In macular degeneration, there seems to be a destructive response to irritation. When the retina becomes inflamed, the repair mechanism is not normal and may cause more loss of this vital tissue. This is like having a bad mechanic work on your car. Not only will it not be fixed, but the mechanic damages the car so that it's worse than when you brought it in.

Dietary supplements that protect cells from various types of irritation also protect the rods and cones. These concepts were behind the AREDS (Age-Related Eye Disease Study). They demonstrated that certain vitamin supplements caused a significant benefit in AMD. This will be discussed later on. If you want to read it now, you can skip ahead to the nutrition chapter.

Light Damage

When light hits the back of the eye, it can sometimes hurt it. Ultraviolet (UV) light can create something called free radicals. These are harmful chemicals created when light strikes a molecule and causes a reaction within the surrounding areas. These reactions occur regularly in the very center of the back of the eye. The eye is designed to take all incoming light and focus it into this one tiny area. Fortunately, the eye has defenses against these harmful chemical reactions. Part of the body's defense against light rays involves pigments, the chemicals that cause color. Higher pigmentation levels cause more resistance to this harmful effect of light. This is one of the reasons why paler skinned people with lighter colored eyes may be more at risk from the damaging effects of light.

Wet and Dry Macular Degeneration

In general, macular degeneration has two forms. When there is a slow loss of function associated with the changes mentioned above, a person is described as having "dry" macular degeneration. In some patients with AMD there can be a profound sudden loss of vision. This usually means they have made the conversion from the mild "dry" form to the severe "wet" form of macular degeneration. "Wet" macular degeneration implies the growth of new blood vessels below the macula that shouldn't be there. These abnormal vessels leak fluid and distort the structure of the macula. Through this distortion they cause severe decreased vision. The second form of macular degeneration usually occurs after the first has been going on for a while. So, the "wet" category characteristically occurs in the presence of the "dry" form.

Conversion from Dry to Wet AMD

When a person changes from dry to wet macular degeneration, he or she will have a sudden severe change in the ability to see detail. This happens because new blood vessels grow under the retina in the presence of the pre-existing degeneration. These new blood vessels distort the shape of the back of the eye and consequently distort vision. They leak fluid and blood, which distorts the shape of the retina and kills retinal cells.

Wet macular degeneration is much less common than dry. Both can cause permanent bad vision. Approximately 90% of people simply have the dry form of macular degeneration, while around 10% will have the more severe wet form. So only

10% of patients with age-related macular degeneration will grow abnormal blood vessels under their retinas and progress from the dry to the wet form of AMD.

Risk Factors for Macular Degeneration

- Age (over 55 years old)
- Light-colored eyes and hair (Scandinavian ancestry)
- Smokers (the larger the amount smoked, the greater the risk)
- A family history of macular degeneration
- Long-term exposure to ultraviolet light and blue light (the wavelength just above ultraviolet), which includes sunlamps as well as regular light
- Obesity (high body mass index)
- Diabetes
- High levels of fat in your blood
- High blood pressure
- Certain medications – Anti-inflammatory and antacid.

Note: Losing weight and decreasing smoking can reduce the chance of visual loss.

How to Diagnose AMD

There are many ways to diagnose AMD. First, the visual acuity is often reduced. Visual acuity is the ability to distinguish detail. It is measured according to an eye chart. People with dry macular degeneration may see anywhere on this chart. They may see the bottom line (20/20 vision) or they may only see the giant letter E (20/400 vision).

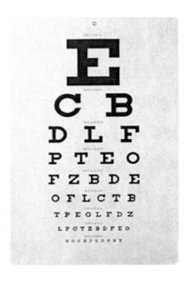

In general, a person with mild dry AMD tends to see somewhere toward the bottom of the eye chart. Eye doctors think of this as relatively good vision. Patients, however, often disagree. Many think that anything worse than perfect is poor vision. The eye doctor response is that a person with an intermediate level of vision can be quite functional in terms of visual tasks. So, while many people think that macular degeneration means eventual blindness, it does not. Most commonly, people with AMD have only moderate visual loss.

Another way to diagnose macular degeneration is through the Amsler grid.

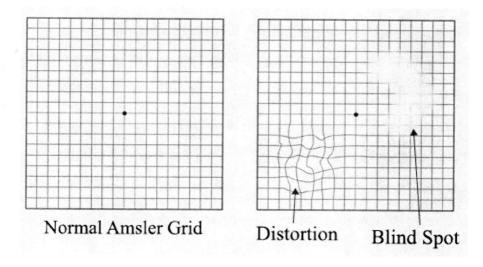

Normal Amsler Grid   Distortion   Blind Spot

Some of the potential changes on the grid which may indicate conversion from dry to wet macular degeneration.

Macular degeneration tends to cause some areas on this grid to be lost or distorted. A person who has macular degeneration should check this grid daily. In mild dry macular degeneration there may be missing spots, faded areas, or slight distortion in a small part of the very center of vision. These areas should be mapped on the grid. When daily self-testing is done, one should check to make sure these areas have not changed.

To perform this test, one should wear the correct glasses for reading. The grid should be held at the normal reading distance in good light. Alternatively covering each eye, look at the center dot and check for missing or distorted areas. If present, these areas should be mapped. Each day one should check to see if these areas have changed. If there is a change, one should seek care as soon as possible. This may indicate a change from dry to the more severe wet form of macular degeneration. If you are caught without a grid, a modified form of this test can be performed. This is done by covering one eye and looking at the nose of someone's face. If all parts of that person's face are visible, the test result is normal. If, however, a portion of the person's face is missing – for example, one eye or chin – the result is abnormal. This can also be done by looking at yourself in the mirror and alternatively covering each eye.

Despite the fact that vision may be normal in a person with macular degeneration, an examination by an ophthalmologist is an important procedure for any person over 55 years of age. This should involve dilation of the pupils and evaluation of the macula with a biomicroscope. A person will not know if he has AMD without an eye exam. If you are over 55 and have normal vision with early macular degeneration, you may want to lose weight and stop or reduce smoking to improve your chances of good vision.

There are other ways of determining the presence and degree of macular degeneration. One of them is through a test that uses special cameras to take microscopic pictures of the macula. A fluorescein angiogram involves the injection of dye into the bloodstream and taking special photographs of the macula as the dye arrives in the eye. As the dye circulates through the bloodstream and eventually to the eye, the blood vessels in the retina stand out when observed with a special light. There are characteristic pictures defining the type of macular degeneration in this test.

Ocular coherence tomography (OCT) is the creation of a cross-section image of the retina using reflective light collected by a computer. It can show structural abnormalities without making an injection. All of these methods should be considered when a person is evaluated for macular degeneration.

Treatments for Wet Macular Degeneration

Again, when a person with pre-existing dry macular degeneration develops a sudden severe visual loss, it usually means the disease is converting from the mild dry form to the serious wet form.

Wet macular degeneration involves the growth of new blood vessels below the macula. These blood vessels distort the shape of the macula simply by their presence and through the leakage of fluids through their abnormal vessel walls. This will result in a change of the structure and function of the back of the eye. Consequently the vision is suddenly reduced. The treatments mentioned below are designed to eliminate these vessels.

The oldest form of treatment is called photocoagulation. An argon laser is used to destroy the new vessels and the overlying macula. A successful treatment of this type causes the destruction of an area just outside the very center of vision. This causes a person to continue to be able to read but with a black spot just next to a word. The usefulness of photocoagulation is limited because in about 90% of wet AMD, new blood vessels grow below the very center of the macula. In these cases, photocoagulation causes a dense black spot in the center of vision. Even when the blood vessels grow to the side and central vision can be maintained 50% of the time, the blood vessels grow back anyway and destroy central vision.

The next treatment developed for new blood vessels was photodynamic therapy (PDT). In this treatment, a chemical is injected into the bloodstream, and then light is shined into the eye and absorbed by this chemical to create heat, which destroys the new abnormal blood vessels. The problem with this therapy is that the ultimate visual loss is usually the same. However, it does slow the progression of visual loss.

Part of the mechanism the body uses to make new blood vessels involves the production of chemical messengers. This is the way the body tells certain areas to make new blood vessels. Newer treatments for wet macular degeneration involve suppressing this message. An important messenger of this type is vascular endothelial growth factor (VEGF). Without this message, new vessels are not created. It may be that abnormal vessels, which have already formed, will disappear. This disappearance accounts for the improvement in vision some people get on these VEGF inhibitors. These are naturally occurring chemicals. They are a critical part of the development of new blood vessels. Injection of this chemical into the eye causes the deactivation of new blood vessel growth. If the blood vessels are stopped from forming with this treatment, they cannot distort the shape of the macula or leak fluid. So the vision stops getting worse, and it often improves. The trouble is that often the vessels grow again. Then we simply keep giving these injections. Monthly injections are much better than the permanent inability to read!

At the time of this writing, anti-VEGF treatments are new and very exciting for eye doctors. For the first time we have something that slows the conversion from the dry to wet form of macular degeneration. In some cases, vision may be improved. This is an area of active scientific advancement. Many new treatments for macular degeneration are being developed.

It is important to understand that these treatments should be customized to the individual. Treatments are constantly changing. Everyone is different. Only after consultation with an ophthalmologist can you know the correct way to take care of your individual situation.

Nutritional Supplementation for ARMD

I like to be as scientific as possible when discussing vitamin supplementation and macular degeneration. There will always be more that we do not know than we do know. Victims of macular degeneration are often surprised and frustrated to find out how little is known about the causes and treatment of this blinding condition.

Age-Related Eye Disease Studies

There was a series of studies that provided a lot of useful information about macular degeneration. It examined the effect of specific vitamin supplements on the loss of vision from macular degeneration. These authors demonstrated a clear benefit from a specific amount of vitamins A, E, C, calcium, and the minerals zinc and copper. These improvements, however, are only related to reduction of the chance for someone to convert from dry to wet macular degeneration. Patients on specific amounts of these supplements had a 25% decrease in the chance of conversion from mild dry to severe wet macular degeneration. They also demonstrated an increased risk of conversion to wet macular degeneration in smokers and overweight people. So if a person has macular degeneration, he can improve his chances of good vision by losing weight and decreasing or stopping smoking.

This specific set of vitamin supplements, located in the table below, is proven to reduce the chance of progression of this disease. The trouble is that excess doses of certain vitamins, especially A, D, E, and K, can cause toxic levels, resulting in very powerful side effects.

AREDS (Age-Related Eye Disease Study) Formula

Vitamin A (100% as beta carotene)	**75,000 IU**	**15 mg**
Vitamin C (Ascorbic acid)		**500 mg**
Vitamin E (dl-alpha tocopheryl acetate)	**400 IU**	**180 mg**
Calcium (dicalcium phosphate)		**132 mg**
Zinc (zinc oxide)		**80 mg**
Cooper (cupric oxide)		**2 mg**

Vitamin supplementation at the level of dry AMD is controversial. The AREDS study doesn't show a decreased rate of progression in cases of low-risk macular degeneration. Because there should be no harm with supplementation and because it is shown to reduce the chance of progression in more advanced cases, some ophthalmologists recommend vitamin supplements even before patients meet the criteria of more advanced disease. This is not a scientific recommendation, but at least we are doing something. We don't have proof that it works, but good nutrition never hurts!

Omega-3 Fatty Acids

Omega-3 fatty acids may offer protection against macular degeneration. They capture the harmful chemicals caused by UV light. They may also prevent heart disease. Omega-3 fatty acids are found in most coldwater fish. They can also be taken in tablets. See more of this in the chapter "Nutrition and the Eye."

Toxicity Levels in Vitamin Supplementation
Vitamin A

This vitamin plays an essential role in vision, growth, and

development. Vitamin A toxicity can occur with long-term consumption of 100.000 IU (20 mg+) or more per day. The symptoms of vitamin A toxicity include accumulation of water in the brain (hydrocephalus), vomiting, and fatigue.

Vitamin C

The tolerable upper intake level of vitamin C for adults is 2000 mg. More than this is associated with formation of kidney stones.

Zinc (Zn)

More than 90 milligrams daily of zinc can be toxic. This dose and higher was associated with increased hospital admissions for genitourinary problems, vomiting, and diarrhea.

Vitamin E

This vitamin may be toxic if taken more than 800 mg per day. High intakes of vitamin E (100 times the recommended level) may interfere with utilization of other fat-soluble vitamins (vitamins A, D, and K).

Copper (Cu)

Copper is a trace mineral. More than 100 mg per day can result in anemia. It is used in the AREDS study to help the absorption of zinc.

Often patients are taking other multivitamins (e.g., Centrum Silver From A to Zinc®). They don't know if they should continue their usual vitamin supplements. The response is that toxic levels should be avoided. To address this issue of vitamin intake, fill out the calculator below to incorporate your daily multivitamin with the specific vitamins and minerals in the AREDS recommendation.

Dosage Calculator for AREDS Vitamins

Add the amount you already take in your daily vitamin supplementation to the AREDS dose. Make sure the total amount of each vitamin is below toxic level.

AREDS Amount + Daily Supplementation

= Total Daily Dose

	Column I	Column II	Column III	Column IV toxic levels
Vitamin A	18,640 IU	+_____	=_____	100,000 IU = 20mg
Vitamin C	500 mg	+_____	=_____	2,000 mg
Vitamin E	(180 mg) 400 IU	+_____	=_____	1,600 IU = 720mg
Zinc	80 mg	+_____	=_____	90 mg
Copper	2 mg	+_____	=_____	100 mg

If you take multivitamins in addition to the AREDS formula of vitamins, read your bottle and enter the amount of vitamins in column II. Add column I to column II and then enter the sum into column III. Compare column III to column IV for each supplement. If column III is greater than column IV, you are taking too much of this vitamin or mineral. Consult your doctor in this case.

I suggest the use of ICaps® AREDS formula, specifically the ICaps® with the antioxidants lutein and zeaxanthin. This should be available in most drug stores without a prescription, as well as the ICaps® MV, a formula free of vitamin A for those who should avoid beta-carotene.

Lutein and zeaxanthin are present in the macula of the human retina, as well as the human crystalline lens. They may play a role in protection against age-related macular degeneration.

Smokers

Smokers should simply not take vitamin A or anything labeled as beta-carotene. Most diets will probably provide enough of the minimum recommended. However, in order to get a balanced intake of antioxidants and vitamins from the AREDS formula, smokers should take ICaps® MV. Any additional amount could increase the risk of lung cancer. We all know that the risk is much higher in smokers anyway. Lung cancer is often fatal. It is of course very hard to maintain normal vision after death. So in general the recommendation is to stay alive. If people want to live and see, they should consider not smoking, achieving ideal body weight, and maintaining a diet rich in fresh fruits and raw vegetables (I wish I could do that).

Lung cancer is really sad!

If something increases the risk of lung cancer, just don't do it. In medical school, I learned that if it feels good or tastes good, just don't do it. The more you like something, the worse it seems to be for you. However, most of us cannot live this way. Smoking is as statistically difficult to stop as heroin. So, if you are going to smoke, don't take vitamin A (beta-carotene). Even if you have macular degeneration, it is better to lose your central vision than to die of lung cancer. Remember, however, that cutting down improves your chances of both life and vision.

Sun Protection

When I was still a resident training to be an eye M.D., I went to a national conference of ophthalmology. Approximately ten thousand eye doctors attended this conference. As I waited for a friend outside in the bright sunshine, I was amazed by the fact that thousands of ophthalmologists came out into the bright sunlight and every single one put on dark tinted sunglasses. I thought at the time that this was a clear testimonial to what ophthalmologists think in terms of eye protection.

When people ask me what kind of sunglasses they should get for protection against ultraviolet light, my response is that there was a study done on how effective sunglasses were in blocking out ultraviolet light. There was no relationship between cost and effectiveness. In fact, many cheap sunglasses that are not polarized are very effective in blocking UV light. I suggest buying any kind of sunglasses. When my patients ask me if they should wear sunglasses, I always say yes. This is especially true in Southern California, where my practice is located. Personally, whenever I am in the sunlight, I wear sunglasses. Although it has not been proven scientifically, I think it will reduce my chances of getting cataracts or macular degeneration. Also, it feels good and looks cool.

Living with Macular Degeneration

Macular degeneration involves the deterioration or breakdown of the macula. This is the portion of the eye responsible for all detail vision, both near and far. If one has severe degeneration and loses the function of the macula, it will be difficult to do any activity that involves detail vision. This includes reading, threading a needle or a fishing hook, and seeing signs while driving.

Advice on Reading with Macular Degeneration

When people have moderate visual loss from dry macular degeneration, they often are able to read in certain conditions. The idea is to use every advantage to see while reading. Start by having the correct glasses. These glasses should not be progressive bifocals. Progressive lenses introduce distortion. A person with macular degeneration should use reading glasses or regular bifocals with a line. Non-progressive lenses create the least distortion. This type of lens is designed to focus light at a specific distance. The patient should understand that there will be one distance where things are in the best focus. This distance should be known by the reader. It is important to place the reading material at exactly the right focusing point.

Get the light just right.

The correct lighting is critical. In macular degeneration, too much or too little light is bad, for it can reduce vision. The amount of reading light required is different for each person. I like to recommend that a person get a moveable light. If a light is connected to a moveable arm, by moving the light toward and away from the reading material, it will be easier to determine which intensity is just right for the degree of one's macular degeneration. Some people think that fluorescent light doesn't work as well as other types of light from incandescent light bulbs or sunlight. Try it all and see what is right for you.

It is also important to make sure there are no other reasons for poor vision. Most commonly, dry eyes and cataracts affect the quality of vision in elderly patients with macular degeneration. In order to optimize reading, visually significant cataracts should be removed. Even if there is only a moderate improvement in reading vision from cataract surgery, it is still usually worth the effort. It is sometimes difficult to explain to people with macular degeneration and cataracts that they will go through a surgery for a minor improvement. A slight improvement in vision, however, can take a person from not quite being able to read print to a moderate reading ability. In my opinion, this is a valuable effort.

Don't forget to blink.

An often unrecognized factor affecting reading in patients with macular degeneration is "dry eyes." In general, "dry eyes" means that a person doesn't make as many "all the time" tears as he should. This alone can cause trouble reading. The surface of the eye (the cornea) must be moist to focus well. When a person tries very hard to see, he tends to blink less. This causes the eyes to become dry by not blinking. If someone starts without an adequate tear film, they make their vision worse by concentrating on their vision. Elderly patients tend to have dry eyes. This may cause dramatic problems when they read, even without macular degeneration. Artificial tears and frequent blinking are some of the potential ways to moisturize the surface of the eye and optimize reading vision. There are also medications to improve tear production.

If all possible advantages are used, a person with some visual loss from macular degeneration may often be able to read quite well. The light should be correct for the individual, cataracts should be removed if they interfere with reading, the correct glasses should be used, reading material should be placed at the best distance for these glasses, and the eyes should be moist.

Visual Aids for Macular Degeneration

For people with severe visual loss from AMD, visual aids should be used. The concept behind these tools is to enlarge the words so much that the letters can be seen even though there is a blank spot in the middle of vision. The first step in this direction is usually a "hand magnifier." These magnifiers may come with attached lights. This way you can get the light just right for your individual degree of degeneration.

The position of this magnifier related to the reading material is critical. It has to be in just the right place. Even when magnification is set up perfectly, the vision will still not be perfect. This often leads to frustration, misunderstanding, and suffering. Some form of visual function can usually be achieved. I think it is a victory if these visual aids can be used to pay bills; that way, people can stay independent. Many other aids are available to keep people independent. There are special low-vision centers that provide consultation about these valuable tools.

Domestic Activities with Macular Degeneration

Without central vision, it will be hard to see someone's features, write a check, dial a phone, and read labels of medications or instructions. Although living with macular degeneration seems difficult, many patients have found ways to get around the problem. This can be done by ordering special phones with larger numbers, listening to books on CD or tape (audio books are available in public libraries and bookstores), and reading large print books. You can ask friends and relatives to send return-address stickers so you don't have to address letters.

Driving with Macular Degeneration

The aging process is frightening. We all will go through a progressive deterioration of every part of our bodies. The deterioration of certain parts is more frightening than others. In general, my patients are most concerned with vision, mental faculties, and mobility. These abilities are all involved in driving. The loss of a person's driver's license has a profound impact on lifestyle in Southern California. This is why I often find myself struggling to maintain driving vision for my patients. They come to me with moderate visual loss after failing the vision test at the department of motor vehicles. Often there are two or three factors contributing to their decreased vision. Because one of my principle jobs as an ophthalmologist is to maintain overall visual function, often I find myself battling numerous small factors which add up to cause just enough vision loss to impair driving.

A good example of this is the story of J. S. He is a very nice retired engineer. His vision was below driver's license requirements in California. He was anxious to maintain his independence and activity level. He approached the problem of visual loss as he would a difficult engineering problem. He took careful notes during our discussion of each of his visual problems. Then we approached each problem with a good understanding on his part of both the problems and solutions. By removing his cataracts, moisturizing his dry eyes, and giving him exactly the right glasses, we achieved 20/40 vision in one eye and 20/50 in the other. He passed his driving test and currently has a valid California driver's license.

Low-Vision Consultation

There are specialists who work specifically with people with poor vision to help them function. They tend to use optical devices to expand the size of letters. If you have macular degeneration and are having problems functioning, it can't hurt to see one of these specialists. Remember, though, that they will not completely fix macular degeneration. Instead, they help you work around the central visual loss.

Recommendations

Anyone over 55 should be checked for macular

degeneration. People with high-risk AMD should take vitamin supplementation (AREDS formula) if they are not smokers. If recommended by their ophthalmologist, they should check their eyes daily using the Amsler grid, stop smoking, lose weight, and get the right glasses. If there is a change in the Amsler grid, they should be checked within three days.

Story

John Clark is a doctor still in practice near my office. In his seventies, he came to me with moderate visual loss from cataracts and macular degeneration. After cataract surgery and new glasses, he got to 20/40 in both eyes and passed his driving test. I encouraged him to stop smoking, lose weight, and take multivitamins to improve his chances to maintain good vision. I gave him an Amsler grid and told him to report any changes immediately. Of course, he knew he was supposed to stop smoking and lose weight. But knowing and doing are two different things. I often say to my patients: if it feels good or tastes good, DON'T DO IT!

They never seem to listen. Of course, I don't do everything my own doctor tells me. So John kept smoking and suffered progressive visual loss in the very center of his vision from macular degeneration. But he didn't want to stop driving or doing surgery. I encouraged him to stop driving and operating, but for a while he continued. Later, I heard stories about his inability to see needles and the tips of other sharp objects while operating. Not only could he not see the instruments, but he had a hard time identifying the anatomy he was dissecting. When he passed a needle, he would recover it by feel. Of course, this placed him at risk for various blood-borne infections. At first, his assistant surgeons would take over for him. Then, when they noticed he was too dangerous to patients and to the assistant surgeons themselves, they refused to operate with him. Eventually he was convinced to give up his surgical privileges.

But that didn't stop him from driving. He lived on a winding road in the hills. One day while driving home, he struck a car coming out of a driveway. The way I heard the story, he was driving home around sunset and came around a corner. The sun was directly in his eyes. The car was coming out of a shaded driveway. Luckily, it was a low-speed collision and no one was hurt.

After this incident, he hired a driver. The positive side of this story is that after he gave up surgery and driving, he was able to practice medicine on a limited basis. I heard stories that during patient interviews he would bring out a large magnifying glass and a flash light. It made complete sense to me that he could practice medicine within certain limits. Mental ability is not affected by the loss of central vision. The thinking aspect of medical practice could be done quite well by someone without central vision. In fact, his experience of a long, full life and practice is a treasure that should not be lost.

Story

Ann Doyle is an 81-year-old woman who had cataract surgery ten years ago. She had a very mild macular degeneration. I placed her on vitamin ICaps®. Her vision then was 20/20. She had been on the vitamins for two years when she came in complaining of sudden severe decreased vision in one eye.

Ann Doyle agreed to let me tell her story. She was interviewed specially for this book by Marina Marin.

She lost her vision to the level of legal blindness (20/200). The point about this is that we want to see these patients within about three days of the beginning of this problem. The longer they wait, the harder it is to get the vision back, and it may not be possible.

"At first the right eye was very bad. My vision had wavy lines and I could see a black spot in the middle of the images. I think I caught it in time. Dr. May had put me on vitamins long before my eyes got worse."

Doyle received injections of anti-VEGF medications. Three months later, she recovered her vision to level 20/30, which is good enough to drive a car.

Pictures were taken of Ann's eyes, and it was decided she needed anti-VEGF injections. She has had five injections so far.

"I usually go see Dr. May two days after the injections. He wants to see how this treatment is going to result. Now the wavy lines are almost clear. I just love that doctor."

Ann Doyle is paraplegic and lives alone in Wittier. She drives but avoids the night traffic, except on the Fourth of July, when she drove to Dana Point to watch the fireworks at the beach.

Points about This Story

1. The window of opportunity for the use of anti-VEGF drugs is around three days. After that time, the chance of restoring vision goes down. So don't delay. See your ophthalmologist.

2. Even though she was taking the AREDS formula vitamins, she developed wet macular degeneration. So it is still important to check your eyes with the Amsler grid daily.

3. Even if you get AMD in one eye, it can still happen in the other.

4. She didn't give up. She continued to go to her doctor's appointments. Hooray for Ann! Because of her persistence, she sees well in both eyes.

Chapter 4

Dry Eyes

Your tears are evaporating before your eyes.

Baseline Tear Secretion

From moment to moment as an eye blinks, it is bathed in a river of tears. The muscular contraction of each blink pumps fluid across the eye. Each blink causes the release of new tears onto the eye from the lacrimal (tear production) gland. At the same time, closure of the lids pushes tear fluid off the surface into the tear-collection system and then into a reservoir called the nasolacrimal sac. With each blink, this reservoir is emptied into the nose to make way for incoming tear flow.

The eye is bathed in a river of tears.

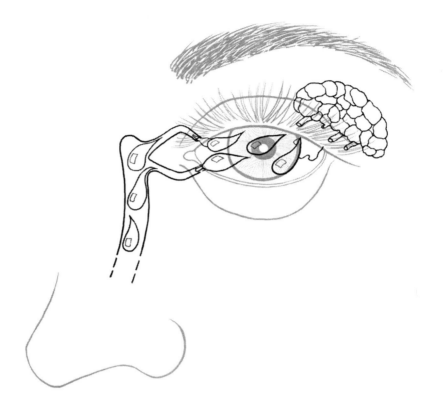

The blink mechanism acts like a pump. It forces fluid out of the lacrimal gland and onto the surface of the eye. Also, blinking forces fluid off the eye and into the tear-collecting system. Then the movement of blinking muscles forces fluid out of the tear-collecting system into the nose.

As if that wasn't complicated enough, what we call "tears" actually have a chemical structure with three layers. The bottom layer is made of a sticky mucous-like layer attached to the ocular surface. The middle layer is made of salt water. This saline layer flows across the mucous layer, washing away potentially harmful or irritating substances. The outermost layer is made of an oily substance. Just like oil in an oil and vinegar salad dressing, it stays above the watery layer. This oily layer stops the salt water layer from evaporating. By itself, this oil is toxic to invading germs. These three layers are like three walls protecting the eye from infectious particles. To even get to the ocular surface, they have to pass through each barrier. Normally, an eye is covered with this complex fluid. If any one of these layers is not present in sufficient amounts, the eye hurts and the vision suffers.

How does the cornea stay wet?

The thing about the cornea (the front of the eye) is that it is a vertical surface. How would one keep a wall-like structure wet? Well, you could run a waterfall across it from top to bottom. But that would take a lot of water, and it would have to be evenly distributed. The flow would have to be just right. If there were too much flow, the waterfall would overflow the drain, spill where it doesn't belong, and waste a precious resource. Too little flow, and parts would dry out. The eye solves this fluid distribution problem by blinking and holding fluid up with the lower lid.

Blinking causes the release of tears and their uniform distribution across the ocular surface. For someone to be comfortable, they must blink well. What? You might say that everybody can blink. We all know how, right? It's not hard. Well, actually, some people don't blink often enough. And some don't blink well enough. Sometimes the action of blinking doesn't completely distribute tears over the ocular surface. If one doesn't blink frequently enough, there is no chance to put more tears on the eye. The fluid eventually evaporates, and the eye dries out.

Age affects blinking.

As a person gets older, everything gets looser. This applies to the connections that hold the lid against the eye. A loose muscle may not do its work as well. These loose connections allow the lower lid to fall out of position. This is easy to see in other people. The next time you are with an elderly person, first look to see if you can see white below the colored part of their eyes. If you can see that, it means their lower lids are out of position. They are most likely to droop because of a progressive loosening of the tendons that hold the lower lid up.

Then observe if the upper lid actually comes into contact with the lower lid when the person blinks. If the lower lid is droopy, the upper lid doesn't chase it down into the new position during a blink. This creates an area where the act of blinking doesn't completely cover the eye with tears. This band of dryness can cause pain and blurred vision.

This test doesn't work if you tell people what you are doing. If you do, they usually immediately make a voluntary complete blink. This is done as a conscious effort. If they think about complete closure, they can do it. The trouble is, as a doctor you can't just tell someone to blink better. There are too many other things to do during the day. People can't spend every waking moment concentrating on blinking.

When this process becomes more severe, the lids may not close during sleep. In these situations, when a person sleeps, his eyes remain open. Luckily, the eyes tend to turn up and out during sleep so the cornea (the more sensitive clear part in front of the eye) is usually still covered. But even exposing the lower eyeball to air all night can be painful. These people often wake up with pain and tearing every morning.

The lower eyelid holds the tears up onto the cornea (the first of two lenses in the camera of the eye). If the lower eyelid droops or turns out, tears fall down into the space between the eye and the lid. This causes pooling of fluid where it is not needed. Also, the cornea suffers because it doesn't get enough tears.

Blink rate (blinks per minute) decreases in certain situations. Concentration tends to reduce blink rate. This can lead to a negative spiral. When people don't see well, they tend to concentrate more on their vision. This concentration leads to a reduced blink rate. That causes their eyes to dry out. Their vision then gets worse. This can cause any reason for visual loss to get worse. Eye doctors see this all the time during the examination for glasses.

When I was a new eye doctor, I didn't understand why some people were easy to examine for glasses and others weren't. Sometimes I would show patients different options for lens power and they would choose the right ones immediately. Other times, no matter how many different lenses I tried, I couldn't figure out what power lenses would make them see the way I knew they should. First I thought it was me. As a beginner, I thought that there was something I was missing.

Well, it turns out that there was something I didn't know.

The patients were trying too hard! They were concentrating so much that they weren't blinking enough. This caused their eyes to dry out. Then their vision would actually get worse. Also, the correct glasses lens power would continually change. So my testing wouldn't work. The patient would get frustrated, and so would I. I often hear new patients saying that their previous eye doctor got mad at them for not giving the "right answers" to their questions about which lenses worked better. Of course, these people were trying very hard, concentrating and therefore not blinking. The answer to the eye doctor's questions about which lenses made them see better constantly changed as the eyes became more and more dry. Now when I do this test, I am constantly encouraging my patients to keep blinking during the exam.

What to Do about Droopy Lower Lids and Incomplete Blink

The lower lids can be lifted along with the cheeks. This usually puts the lower edge of the lid higher. This specific surgery is usually done by an ophthalmic plastic surgeon. That is an ophthalmologist who specializes in the medicine and surgery of the area around the eye.

This mid-facelift also has cosmetic benefits. (See the chapter "Plastic Surgery.")

"But doctor, if my eyes are dry, why am I always crying?"

There are actually two different types of tears: baseline tears and reactive tears. Reactive tears are produced in response to eye irritation or severe emotion. Not having enough baseline tears may cause the release of the reactive tears. If not enough fluid washes the eye, it becomes dry. Then particles like pollen and dust, instead of flowing away, land on the surface of the eye and cause irritation and allergic reactions. In response to this irritation, the reactive type of tear is released. These types of tears are held in a reservoir inside the lacrimal gland. They are released in a flood and overwhelm the normal drainage system. They spill over the edge of the lid onto the face and cause tearing. This type of tear is also the type of tear released in severe emotional reactions. Certain amounts of these tears do flow down the drain and cause a runny nose.

Symptoms of Dry Eyes: Vision Fluctuation, Eye Irritation, and Tearing

In order to remain clear, the surface of the eye must be covered by moisture. As a child I used to have staring contests with my friends. We would try to look at each other without blinking. This caused pain, decreased vision, and eventually reactive tearing. We were causing the tear film to evaporate. This alone resulted in decreased vision. Particles normally suspended in the tear film would contact the surface of our eyes and cause pain. In response to this pain, reactive tears would flood the surface of our eyes and spill out onto our cheeks. As young boys, we would then shout out, "Ha, ha, you're crying!" This is exactly what happens in a patient with baseline tear deficiency (dry eyes). But of course nobody laughs. At least, not to your face.

Why do I have dry eyes?

The current thinking about the causes of dry eyes is that chronic inflammation causes progressive damage to the tear-production system. This causes slow reduction of the amount of tears produced. When this happens, people notice a slow worsening of vision, ocular discomfort, and increased tearing from reactive tear production. If this process is not reversed with medicines, the ability to make tears may be permanently lost. How long it will take to permanently lose the ability to make tears? We don't know. There is no way to know if a particular person will get to this point. The individual factors include how much irritation is going on, how dry the eyes are, and age.

Treatments for Dry Eyes

Tear Replacement

Tear replacement with artificial tears washes away inflammatory particles and improves vision and comfort. However, they may not reverse the progressive damage to the tear-production system from chronic inflammation. This progressive damage may be quite advanced at even a very young age.

In my office it is common to see people in their twenties with significant dry eyes. This is scary because they may rapidly progress to a permanent untreatable loss of tearing function. So they might suffer for the rest of their lives with eye irritation and decreased vision without much hope of improvement.

The point is that you don't want to lose the tear-production system. Once it is lost, it is gone. People in this situation will suffer the rest of their lives. Anyone even with moderate dry eyes should try to bring back their lacrimal production system by working with an ophthalmologist.

Plugs

The tear drainage system can be blocked with temporary or permanent plugs. In general, this doesn't hurt. Temporary plugs made of collagen will dissolve naturally in about two weeks. They are commonly used as a test to see if permanent blockage should be performed. Plugs cause the few tears that are made to remain longer on the ocular surface. The permanent types are made of silicone. These silicone implants remain blocking their tear drain for a long time (hopefully years). From time to time, these plugs can be felt. If they cause pain or a scratchy sensation, they are easy to remove in the office. The basic idea here is to try to avoid putting artificial tear eye drops in your eyes constantly and to avoid using an expensive prescription medication.

Treatment with Medicines

Certain medicines may improve tear production. The main medication that does this is Restasis® (Cyclopsporin). This eye drop medication causes rejuvenation of the tear-production system. It can be used as a twice-a-day drop. We think this medicine stops inflammation in the tear-producing glands and promotes recovery of their normal function. Other medicines that inhibit inflammation can also help the lacrimal gland recover and produce more tears. These include steroid eye drops and non-steroidal anti-inflammatory drops.

The trouble with using any specific medicine is that these treatments must be individualized. Each treatment carries potential side effects. How much of a particular medication to use is a judgment call. Risks and benefits must be analyzed for each individual. These are issues that must be discussed with your ophthalmologist.

Omega-3 Fatty Acids

This dietary supplement is one of the things we try when we can't make other treatments work. It contains essential fatty acids found especially in coldwater fish. The American diet is poor in this type of fat. Omega-3 fatty acids are thought to support the cardiovascular system. They have an anti-inflammatory effect on the tear glands and can help the lacrimal glands recover. Also, they might help macular degeneration. (See the nutrition chapter for more information on this nutrient.)

Different Types of Artificial Tears

In general, I tell my patients that artificial tears are essentially all the same, with two important differences: there are preserved and non-preserved tears. There are also thicker and thinner tears. It is actually more complex than that. These tears are made of different amounts of different components. None of these substances is a medicine. So the basic point is that an individual should use whatever works. These eye drops cannot cause serious harm. One type may be more effective than another for a specific individual. Try lots of different types and see what works.

Non-preserved artificial tears come in breakable tubes. They are good for people with very sensitive eyes. It is theoretically impossible for them to cause irritation. The trouble is, they must be carried in a lot of little tubes. One new tube must to be broken each time you put them on your eyes.

Preserved artificial tears come in a bottle. The preservatives usually do not cause irritation. For someone who simply has dry eyes, a bottle is the most convenient way to carry artificial tears. However, if a person is very sensitive to preservatives and has allergic reactions to many things, the non-preserved tears in tubes are better.

The other difference between the two types of artificial tears is the thickness, or viscosity. The thicker the tear, the longer it lasts. However, the thicker the tear, the more it blurs your vision. Individuals will respond differently to these artificial tears. In some, the blur will disappear after seconds, while in others, vision will stay blurry for a longer period of time.

Thinner tears do not last very long but do not blur vision. When my patients ask me which type they should use, I tell them in my Brazilian Portuguese, *"Tudo bom,"* meaning, it is all good. Whatever artificial tear that works for them is good. When they ask me how many times a day they should use the tears, I tell them no more than one thousand times per day. Anything less is fine. Most people with dry eyes do not use tears more than four times a day. This is not enough. I tell my patients that if they have irritation, tearing, or fluctuating vision, they have not used enough artificial tears. So you might ask, "How much should I use them?" The answer is as much as it takes to get your eyes comfortable and your vision stable. Then you might say, "I don't want to use anything on my eyes more than twice a day." The response would be to try various medicines, dietary supplements, or plugs.

Examples of Artificial Tears from Methylcellulose

Preserved	Non-preserved
Refresh Liquigel	**Refresh Celluvisc®**
(1% Methylcellulose)	(1% Methylcellulose)
Refresh Tears	**Refresh Plus Tears**
(0.3% Methylcellulose)	(0.5% Methylcellulose)
Tears Naturale® II	**TheraTears®**
(0.3% Methylcellulose)	(0.25% Methylcellulose)
GenTeal Mild®	**Bion® Tears**
(0.3% Methylcellulose)	(0.3% Methylcellulose)
Visine Tears®	**Optive**
(0.2% Methylcellulose)	(0.5% Methylcellulose)

Methylcellulose Containing Artificial Tears

Optive

This is an artificial tear that attempts to replace the outer lipid layer and the watery layer of the tear film that covers the eye. It has methylcellulose, the classic replacement for the watery layer. In addition to this replacement for the watery layer, glycerin is supposed to replace the outer layer of the tears. This is the lipid layer. Normally this layer acts as a barrier to the invasion of infection. It also slows the evaporation of the watery part of the tear cover of the eye. The company that makes this artificial tear claims that this combination protects the outer layer of the eye from the damage of dryness.

This is a different approach from normal artificial tears. Artificial tears try to replace all three layers of tears with one substance – methylcellulose. This is the standard approach that has worked to a certain degree for years. These new mixed-mechanism approaches may or may not be better than the classic approach of just using methylcellulose. What really matters here is how you individually respond to whatever artificial tear that works for you. None of these drops will hurt you. If you are not allergic to the preservatives of artificial tears, you can use as much of any kind as you want to. My suggestion is that you try a variety of these drops and see what works for you.

Tears Naturale® Forte

This artificial tear tries to replace all three layers of the tears with dextran for the bottom mucous layer, methylcellulose for the middle layer, and glycerine for the top layer.

Tears Naturale® II

This drop tries to replace the bottom two layers with dextran for the bottom and 0.3% methylcellulose for the middle.

Tears Naturale Free®

Tears Naturale Free® is the same as Tears Naturale® II but without preservatives.

GenTeal®

This tear is a low concentration of methylcellulose (0.3%). It is available both preserved and non-preserved.

Visine Tears®

These also have a low concentration of methylcellulose

(0.2%). They have a preservative that does sometimes cause eye irritation. This is benzalkonium chloride, also known as BAK.

Refresh, Refresh Plus, Refresh Liquigel, and Celluvisc

These popular artificial tears are made of methylcellulose only. They have a progressively higher concentration: 0.3% for Refresh, 0.5% for Refresh Plus, and 1.0% for Celluvisc. They are available preserved in bottles and non-preserved in single-use packets. Refresh Liquigel and Celluvisc are the same thing, except that one is in a bottle with preservatives (Refresh Liquigel) and the other is non-preserved in single-use packets (Celluvisc).

TheraTears®

This artificial tear has a very low concentration of methylcellulose (0.2%). That means it is the least likely to blur your vision. It is "hypotonic," meaning that it has a very low salt concentration. This approach is used in other tears because when the tears evaporate on your eyes, they will leave a higher salt concentration. That may be irritating by itself and may slightly damage the surface of the eye.

Artificial Tears without Methylcellulose

Refresh Endura

This is something completely different from the other types of Refresh. It is made from castor oil, polysorbate (a type of sugar), and glycerine.

Systane®

Systane® is a type of artificial tear that doesn't have the standard methylcellulose lubricant. It has two different tear substitutes. They are polyethylene glycol and guar. The idea is that guar replaces the bottom layer of the tears. Remember that tears have three layers. The bottom layer that attaches to the surface of the eye is the mucous layer. This tightly attached layer covers the surface of the eye and allows the watery layer to flow past and take away pollens and invading infectious particles. The guar is a mucous-like substance that supplements or replaces this bottom layer. The polyethylene glycol is supposed to replace the watery layer flowing over the tightly attached mucous layer.

Artificial Tears Made from Polyvinyl Alcohol

Murine® Tears (0.5% polyvinyl alcohol)

HypoTears® (1.0% polyvinyl alcohol)

Tears Again® (1.5% polyvinyl alcohol)

Akwa Tears® (1.5% polyvinyl alcohol)

These artificial tears have different concentrations of tear substitute. This means the ones with the higher concentrations will be thicker, make your eyes more blurry, and last longer. Lower concentrations will let your vision stay clearer when you first put them in, but will not last as long.

Artificial Tears Made from Glycerin

Computer Eye Drops (1.0% glycerin)

Moisture Eyes (0.3% glycerin and 1.0% propylene glycol)

Advice on Choosing Artificial Tears

Try methylcellulose first. This is the standard type of tear. If this type of tear doesn't work, try a thicker, more concentrated methylcellulose. If these still don't work, try some of the mixtures. If they sting, try the non-preserved variety.

Daily Tearing Cycles

At certain times of the day and with certain activities, the eyes can become dryer. There is a daily tear-production cycle. Eyes naturally become dryer late at night. In the morning, tear production is at its greatest.

When I was a college student, I would notice decreased vision, eye irritation, and tearing while studying hard after midnight. I would say to my study partners, "My eyes are tired. I have to stop studying and go to sleep." But my eyes were not tired; they were simply dry due to the time of the day. Another factor back then may have been stress. Adrenaline is released in times of anxiety. This hormone causes the eyes to open wider. If it is late at night, fewer tears are made. The tears that are released onto the eye are more easily evaporated because the surface area available for evaporation is greater. If I had known this, I would have used artificial tears. Then I would have been able to stay up even later studying!

Morning Tearing, Eye Irritation, and Blurred Vision

During sleep, one does not blink, and fluid is not forced across the eye. When someone sleeps without producing many tears, particles that fall into the eyes build up in the ocular surface and irritate the eyes. Again, dryness alone irritates the eye. Also, all night long, particles from the lids and lashes may collect on the surface of the eye and cause ocular irritation. When the surface of the eye is irritated, it releases a sticky discharge. This dries and glues the eyelids together. When a person wakes, first he notices that he has to pull his lids apart. Then he notices decreased vision and tearing. The decreased vision is caused by irregularities in the shape of the surface of the eye. Dryness and physical irritation from particles irritate the cornea. Tiny particles may cause microscopic scratches. The eye responds by creating local areas of swelling. These microscopic scratches and areas of swelling create an irregular surface. Because the cornea is a lens that actually focuses light, when this lens becomes irregular, focusing is irregular. Then vision becomes blurry. After a person has been awake for a while, by blinking many times, tears are pumped across the surface of the eye, and these particles are washed away. Vision clears, and the eyes become more comfortable. Vision improves because the cornea goes back to its normal shape and consequently focuses better.

When people tell me they cannot open their eyes in the morning, I pause and then ask them if they have a crow bar at home. Puzzled, they usually answer with a cautious "Yes." Then I say, "Okay, just use that to open your eyes. Problem solved."

What else can I help you with?

People with this problem may want to put the thickest type of artificial tears on their eyes before sleeping. These are lubricating eye ointments. They form a barrier overnight so that these particles from the lids do not actually touch the eye and cause irritation. (Examples of lubricating ointments include Lacri-Lube®, DuoLube®, and Refresh PM®.) These ointments are over-the-counter, meaning they do not require a prescription. They are hard to use during the day because they make vision blurry. They are best applied just before bed.

Chilled artificial tears can be very comforting. Just the temperature change reduces ocular irritation and pain. Once again, because dry eyes are a result of chronic irritation, cold may reduce inflammation, improve comfort, and reduce dryness.

Lubricant Ointments
• **Refresh PM® ointment**
• **Tears Naturale® P.M.**
• **Lacri-Lube® ointment**
• **Allergan Refresh PM® Lubricant Eye Ointment**
• **GenTeal® Gel**
• **Tears Again Night & Day gel**
• **Allergan Lacri-Lube® S.O.P.**
• **GenTeal® PM Lubricant Eye Ointment**

Burned-Out Tear Glands

Because inflammation causes progressive damage to the lacrimal system, some people get to the point where their tear-production system gets "burned out." These people can permanently lose the ability to make tears. This usually occurs in older people who have had chronic eye irritation for many years. In these cases, there has been so much damage from chronic inflammation for so long that the tear-production system cannot be recovered. This is one of many reasons to visit an ophthalmologist before eye irritation has been going on for too long.

There is no nobility in suffering. Many people stay away from doctors at all costs. If you have chronic eye irritation, something should be done. The problem is that treatment of this kind of problem can be difficult, time-consuming, and frustrating for both doctor and patient. Treatment for dry eyes often involves addressing incurable underlying chronic problems like ocular allergies, acne rosacea, rheumatoid arthritis, or chronic blepharitis.

Acne rosacea is a disease that makes a person's own tears irritate their eyes. Blepharitis is a disease involving the excessive growth of bacteria on the eyelashes. After these incurable causes of long-lasting eye irritation are controlled, the dry eye problem can be addressed.

Once the underlying causes of irritation are controlled, the lacrimal gland can be rehabilitated with Restasis® (cyclosporin). There are other types of medication that can be used to promote tearing by inhibiting inflammation, but they usually cannot be used on a long-term basis. Sometimes we eye doctors may start someone on a few different types of drops, expecting to change to a longer-term treatment later.

This reminds me of one of my patients, a very nice lady who not only has dry eyes, but she cannot blink. This causes a lot of burning and tearing. She constantly uses artificial tears. She also uses swim goggles at times during the day and always at night. Swim goggles form a moisture chamber that doesn't allow evaporation of the few tears she makes. We have not taken the ultimate step for dry eyes with her. That is to sew the outer third of her eyelids together. This is another way to form a moisture chamber for the eyes. Although this works quite well, most people would rather not have this disfiguring surgery.

Humidity and Dry Eyes

I love New Orleans. I am always looking forward to my next visit. What happened there was a tragedy. Besides the people, music, food, architecture, history, and ambience, I like the humidity. My eyes feel great there. In contrast to Southern California, where I practice, the air in New Orleans is moist and clean. Before I had laser vision correction, when I visited New Orleans I was amazed by how comfortable my eyes were with contact lenses. It wasn't the tears of laughter from the jokes of my friends that made my contact lenses so comfortable late at night. It was the humidity. Yes, eyes dry out at night and make contact lens wear more difficult. In New Orleans I could wear my contact lenses effortlessly until four in the morning. Of course, that was when I was younger and stayed up that late.

Humidity reduces the evaporation of tears from the ocular surface. Now, I don't know of any medical literature saying ocular comfort improves with humidity. But I do know that my fellow ophthalmologists, who were wearing contact lenses at our convention, felt that their eyes were more comfortable. (This is the kind of thing ophthalmologists talk about at conventions.)

Basic chemical principles say that evaporation is reduced by higher humidity. So it makes sense that increasing humidity in the home can improve ocular comfort. Home humidifiers are readily available. They are a good idea for people with severe ocular discomfort from dry eyes as an additional treatment.

Dry eyes make other reasons for ocular discomfort worse. Many diseases are incurable. That includes diseases that cause chronic low-level eye irritation. Although not serious, they can be very annoying. The most common of these are allergies and blepharitis. As mentioned above, these other diseases should be treated both to improve comfort and to reduce their influence toward more dryness. If they are left uncontrolled, they can lead to a negative spiral. For example, in allergies, the dry eyes make the pollens stay on the eye longer. This causes the eye to become dryer. So the next pollens stay on the eye longer and cause even more irritation, resulting in more dryness. This downward spiral continues unless it is somehow disrupted.

Non-medical "Natural" Treatments for Dry Eyes

Some people just don't like to use medications. Since dry eyes will not kill you or make you blind, you could try some "natural" treatments. The following is a list of possible things one could do to improve dry eyes. In general, the idea behind these treatments is to increase humidity and reduce irritation.

Increase Humidity

- To increase humidity, one could buy a humidifier. These are readily available and can be run constantly.

- Before sleeping, a thick lubricating ointment can be used to keep the eye moist at night. As discussed before, this is a time when the eye is dryer. The lack of blinking will reduce the flow of tears across the eye. So at night, lubricating ointment can form a barrier to the particles that constantly fall on the eye from the skin. Also, for people whose eyes may open up just a little bit at night, these ointments can greatly improve comfort.

- Wearing goggles will greatly reduce the evaporation of tears. Some of my patients use these in the home or just at night.

- Because eyes dry out more at night and because concentration can cause reduced blinking, reading at night could be avoided.

- You could move to a more humid climate.

- You could blink more or just keep your eyes closed.

- Most people do not use enough artificial tears. You could put these moisturizing drops in your eyes every hour or more.

Reduce Irritation

- To reduce irritation, lashes can be washed with special soap pads designed for this purpose. This treatment reduces particles on the lids so they don't fall onto the eye.

- Omega-3 fatty acids in fish oils or flax seed oil can reduce inflammation and increase tearing production. The current recommendation is one gram of these oils per day. This treatment may take time to work. Expect to take them for at least a few weeks to cause an effect.

- Air filters can clean the air of pollens. For people with allergies, the reduction of pollens can improve comfort. By reducing inflammation, they can promote tear production.

- Try a variety of artificial tears to see which ones work best for you.

The Story of Paula Bradley

By Paula Bradley

It started out with irritation. I assumed that since I was living in a highly populated city in Texas, pollution was making my eyes itchy. There was also a high probability that winds were blowing pollen from the surrounding states into my area, and I was finally allergic to at least one of them.

I wear soft contact lenses, and, as you other contact lens wearers know, a speck of dirt on the lens can feel like a boulder. I started pumping re-wetting solutions into my eyes, figuring that if the contact lens was getting full of pollution and pollen, it would be natural for my eyes to be constantly red and irritated.

And then there was the air conditioning in the buildings where I worked. Not only was it another great source to dry out my eyes, but it was also a source of major dust, pollutants, etc., as the vents were rarely cleaned.

When I moved to California, things didn't improve – as a matter of fact, they got progressively worse. Commuting to work would cause my eyes to burn and tear up from the exhaust of other cars. I had to stop wearing contact lenses because the air conditioning in the old building I was now working in was turned up high in our area so the folks in accounting wouldn't die of the heat. We wore thermal underwear and sometimes even gloves because of the cold!

Then I found Dr. May. He told me I had conjunctivitis and my eyes were dry not only because of the junk in the air, but at my age, it was common for people's eyes to become dry. He started me on two eye-drop medications, which helped, but I still couldn't wear my contacts.

Finally, he suggested punctal plugs. Inserted in the tear ducts, the plugs keep moisture in the eye from draining out. I had the temporary ones inserted when I lived in Texas, but they didn't seem to do much good. However, in combination with the two eye-drop medications, these plugs made a world of difference. It was a painless procedure (and let me tell you, I'm squirrelly about pain in my eyes). I just felt a little pressure in the corners of my eyes, and then instant relief. We started with the lower plugs, and when they worked so well, he inserted the uppers. I can wear my contacts again, my eyes don't itch or burn, and I don't have to buy re-wetting drops by the caseload.

Here are some points about Paula's story.

There are three main treatments for dry eyes:

- Artificial tears
- Plugs
- Restasis®

Sometimes they work great. When they don't, other potential causes of eye irritation should be considered. The most common are allergies and blepharitis. This combination is discussed more in the chapter titled "The Big Three."

Chapter 5

Cataract

Your internal lenses are cloudy.

Definition

The eye is like a camera. The front is like a lens, and the back is like film. Just behind the colored portion of the eye is the natural lens.

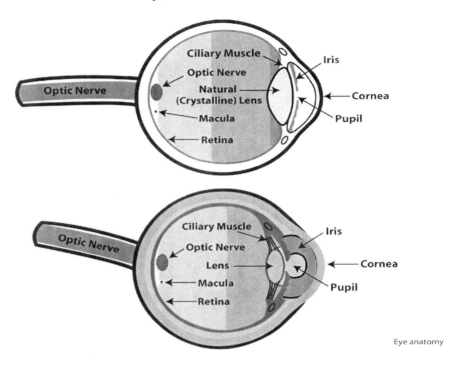

Eye anatomy

The cornea and the lens focus light onto the back of the eye. By opening and closing the pupil, the iris adjusts the amount of light coming into the eye. Focusing by the front of the eye brings light into focus in one tiny part of the retina called the macula. This is where all detail vision starts.

A cataract is cloudiness in the natural lens. This lens focuses light into the retina, and in order to focus, it must be clear. When cloudiness develops in this lens, light is unable to pass through, and the vision gets blurry.

Prevention and Causes

The natural lens is made of protein. We think most cataracts are caused by light. The theory is that as light passes through the lens over the course of a lifetime, it causes damage. We think it does this through free radical formation. What does that mean? When light passes through tissues, it can cause chemical changes. Specifically, the light beams hit the lens and cause the formation of a toxic chemical. This toxin destroys a little bit of the lens before it is captured by the body's natural defense to this problem, called antioxidants. Over a lifetime, these little bits of damage build up. When enough damage happens, the lens loses its clarity. Then you can't see through this cloudy lens (cataract).

Why do some people get them in their forties and others in their eighties? We don't really know for sure. But we think there is a difference in individual defenses against free radicals. This difference is probably caused by a mixture of genetics and environment. Genetics are determined at the moment of conception. You can't do anything about what combination of genes your parents gave you. Some people are less resistant to damage from free radicals because of their individual mix of genes. The other part of this equation is the environment of an individual. The amount of sunlight, the type of sunlight, the foods one eats, and environmental toxins may all be factors in promoting cataracts.

Certain diseases cause cataracts. The most common is diabetes. In this disease, sugar in the blood can increase by huge amounts. When this happens, sugar gets into the lens and causes it to get swollen. That in turn causes damage to the lens and cataract formation.

When I am talking to people about cataracts and they ask if there is anything they can do to prevent them, I usually pause because there is no real scientific evidence that proves the answer. Then I say, "Well, there are some things. The trouble is that they are the same things your other doctors usually bother you about. Cataract formation is less likely if you lose weight and stop smoking. If you are diabetic, keep your blood sugar tightly controlled." Then the patients stop listening because they are tired of hearing the same thing from their other doctors.

Do antioxidant, vitamins, and sunglasses protect you from cataracts?

We don't really know. But it makes sense that they would. Sunglasses can cut down the amount of light hitting your eyes. They can also screen out the types of light more likely to cause damage. Because of its higher energy, ultraviolet light is more likely to damage the eye. It can be specifically filtered out in both sunglasses and regular non-tinted glasses. I personally wear sunglasses as much as I can. I also take antioxidant vitamins when I can remember. But I am a terrible patient. Like most doctors, I believe in the age-old maxim: do as I say, not as I do.

When to Remove

When I was a younger ophthalmologist, I used to tease older ophthalmologists about the mild cloudiness in their lenses. In my experience, this is always present in people over fifty years old. Because I recently celebrated my fiftieth birthday, this is no longer funny. The point is that progressive clouding of the natural lens is seen in everyone after a certain age.

Cataracts become a problem when the best vision with glasses does not allow people to function. Visual function is a very personal thing. Certain jobs require extremely good vision. Airline pilots have such extreme visual requirements that they cannot tolerate the slightest visual loss.

At the other extreme, I once had a patient who was legally blind from cataracts tell me that her vision was fine. When I asked this ninety-year-old what she did during the day, she said, "I like to sit in my rocking chair with my eyes closed and rock back and forth all day long." I answered that although I would like to make her see better, I guess she didn't have any functional visual problems, so there was no need for surgery. "That's right!" she replied.

For each individual, there is a time when removal of cataracts will improve their ability to function depending on their personal needs.

Occasionally I still encounter the attitude that elderly people lose their vision in the natural course of events. Some families used to wonder why I was working to restore vision in an eighty-year-old. From their point of view, I was being unreasonably bothersome asking them to drive their grandfather to his cataract surgery. Couldn't I understand that he was just old? Didn't I know that all old people go blind?

Another question people tend to ask is, "Is there anything that can be done besides surgery for a cataract?" My response is, "No." Then they ask, "What would happen if we don't do any surgery?" The answer is usually one of two things: you will stay the same, or you will get worse. This is a significant point if someone is suffering functional problems. We are all used to problems getting better with time. This problem, however, gets worse.

Sometimes my office is a happiness festival. Everyone coming in exuberantly expressing their great love for me, my staff, and everyone at the surgery center. They can't believe how great their vision is, and how easy the process was.

How soon must it be done? You should make an appointment when vision decreases to the point where it is hard to do whatever is important for you to do. Whether you are going to hunt, sew, or read does not matter. What matters is what is important to you as an individual.

"How long will it take for my cataract to become ripe?" My response is this: "There isn't any fruit inside your eyes, and it doesn't need to be picked at any particular time. It will not rot inside your eye."

"How long will it take?" My serious answer is, "It is impossible to know. Every individual is different in this way." Because a cataract does not harm the eye, it can be left almost forever.

Will there be any problem if we don't do cataract surgery? Well, yes. You will eventually go blind. Most people would consider that a problem. Yes, it is true that if left for a very long time, a cataract could cause inflammation, pain, and glaucoma. But this is very rare.

When considering surgery, it is important to consider the risks and benefits. Some of the serious, potentially blinding problems that can be caused by cataract surgery are infection and retinal detachment. There are also certain forms of bleeding that can cause catastrophic visual loss from cataract surgery. There is a very long list of other less serious potential problems. These problems are rare but should be considered when facing cataract surgery. The potential of these problems is why we don't operate until there is a functional issue. We want some functional benefit in return for our risks. When taken together, only about 3% of cataract surgeries have any problems, and 97% have none at all. About one in one thousand eyes (not people) become blind. Remember, we only operate on one eye at a time. If this horrible event happens, it is usually only in one of two eyes.

Decisions before Surgery

Once the decision is made to have cataract surgery, the next step is to decide which type of intraocular lens to put inside the eye. This is an important decision. There are a few different materials from which these lenses are made. There are also different approaches to how these lenses focus light.

The three different materials intraocular lenses are made of are silicone, polymethylmethacrylate (plastic), and acrylic (another plastic). Currently the most popular type of lens is made of acrylic material. The advantage of this material is that it is foldable. This means it can be rolled up into a tube and inserted into the eye. Then, after it unfolds, it can take the shape of a coin or a disc.

Inserting Intraocular Lens

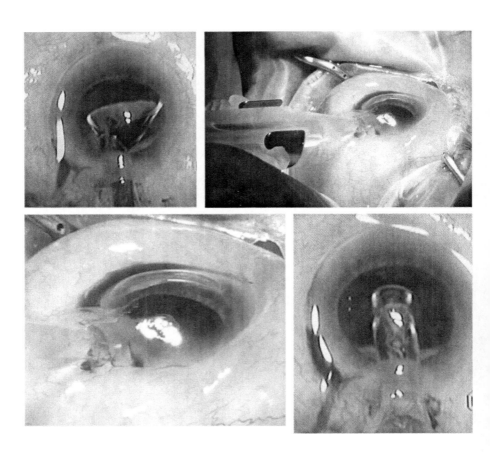

These photographs show a flexible acrylic lens being injected into the eye. It unfolds from a rolled tube into a disc.

Once in the correct position, these lenses can provide high quality focus. Acrylic materials are also quite compatible with the eye. If additional surgeries or laser treatments are needed, this material works well. Polymethylmethacrylate (PMMA) was the standard lens material for many years. This material doesn't cause a reaction with the body. It holds its position well inside the eye, and it's compatible with other types of eye surgery. The trouble with this type of material is that it is rigid. In order to insert this lens, the opening into the eye must be at least six millimeters long (twice as large as usual). Incisions of this size need sutures (stitches). The trouble is that both a larger incision and the stitches for its repair may cause astigmatism. Astigmatism causes the eye to focus poorly. It is usually quite treatable with glasses. But most of my patients would like to see as well as possible without glasses. Currently we don't implant this type of material unless there are problems during the surgery. This type of lens is great for situations where there are worries that the lens may fall out of position.

Silicone lenses are also flexible, and they can be inserted into small incisions. This means astigmatism is less likely. They can provide a very high quality focus. The trouble with these lenses in my own experience is that they can be difficult to deal with if other procedures have to be done later.

Not only is the type of lens material important, the decision of which power lens to implant is critical to the result of the surgery. Before I operate on someone for cataracts, I discuss three options. First there is the option of trying for the best possible distance vision. In this case, if successful, a person can see well in the distance without glasses. They will need glasses to read. But usually they can go without glasses. This is not a big change for most people over forty. They are already used to reading glasses.

Another common approach is monovision. This means that one eye is focused for distance and the other is focused for near. This works surprisingly well for most people. About 25% cannot adapt to this approach, but 75% can.

I am constantly amazed that so many people with monovision do not notice that the eyes are doing different things. It is very common for these people to tell me that they don't realize their eyes are focused for different distances. They say to me, "When I close one eye I notice I can see near but not far. Then when I close the other I notice I can see far but not near. But when both are open I do not notice one is different from the other."

It is important to make sure that a person is a good monovision (one eye near, the other far) candidate before making this a permanent situation. This can be tested quite easily with contact lenses or glasses if a person sees fairly well.

The trouble in a person who sees poorly from cataracts in one or both eyes is that he cannot really try this solution before surgery. We usually find ourselves creating monovision in people who have used this approach for years with contact lenses. Sometimes we create this approach when we can't test it before surgery with the understanding that we can adjust how the eye focuses after surgery with LASIK. (For more on LASIK, see the chapter on refractive surgery.)

Another approach is to create a little bit of nearsightedness in each eye. The end result of this approach is that a person doesn't need glasses indoors. They are focused well for everything inside a room. While driving or watching TV, they may want to wear glasses.

The trouble with all this discussion about exactly how the eye will focus after cataract surgery is that there is variation in how an individual heals after this surgery. Sometimes the eye will be more or less nearsighted than planned because of movement of the lens inside the eye as the artificial lens scars into position.

The surgery sometimes causes astigmatism. This can be another reason for the eye not to see well without glasses. The point is that by choosing the power of the lens that goes inside the eye, we can shoot for a target result. But we are not dealing with a piece of plastic. This living tissue responds in its own unique way. There is individual variation in how close we can come to the planned vision without glasses.

Don't worry! If we get astigmatism, too much farsightedness, or too much nearsightedness after cataract surgery, it can be adjusted. We can usually do LASIK to adjust the focusing power of the eye.

Bifocal Intraocular Lenses

So please remember that when we take a cataract out, we are removing a lens from inside the eye. Without this lens, the eye cannot focus. So we always replace this natural cloudy lens with an artificial lens.

There are two general types of replacement lenses. The classic type of intraocular replacement lens has one focus. This means that it can give you vision either close up or far away. The other type of lens can focus both up close and for distance. Why wouldn't everyone have a lens that would restore both near and far vision in each eye? Well, like so much in life, there are tradeoffs. In a bifocal lens, the light is split into two areas of focus. Normally the way the eye works is to take all the light striking the eye and focus it at one point on the retina.

There are two different approaches to bifocal lenses. The first is a series of circles. They are all centered on the middle of the eye. Some focus the light so you can see up close. They alternate with circles that allow you to see far away. Overall, the light coming into the eye is divided between far vision and near vision. About 75% is focused for distance and 25% is focused for near.

The central part of these lenses gives you faraway vision. Then a ring around this central lens focuses near. Additional rings farther out focus on distance and then near again. You might ask, "If the lens is focused on two places, why don't I see double?" The answer is that while you are looking at distance, there is nothing immediately in front of you. So you don't notice that part of the light is focused for near. By the same token, when you look at something near, you can't see past where you are looking to notice a simultaneous image in focus in the distance.

In my opinion, this concentric circle approach is fine for 90% of cataract surgery patients. The problem is, the vision quality is reduced by about 5% for both distance and near. For someone who doesn't mind not seeing really well either distant or near, these lenses are great. They do have the advantage of allowing someone to see well enough both near and far without glasses. The problem is knowing which patients will like these lenses. There is a dramatic difference in where each of these concentric circles focuses. Because they alternate between near and far, they might create lots of problems with glare. Currently there is no way to test patients before surgery to determine if they will like this approach to vision.

In addition to all these concerns, there is some variation in how we measure the eye. People can be hard to measure. We ophthalmologists have to try to understand exactly how your eye works. We have to know exactly how long it is and how the clear part in the front of your eye (the cornea) focuses. This can be a difficult measurement in a living, breathing, moving, eye-squeezing, imperfect human being. There is some uncertainty in all our measurements. This and individual healing characteristics makes the vision after cataract surgery with any particular intraocular lens somewhat unpredictable. This is why, when I plan one of these surgeries, I tell my patients we will probably do a LASIK procedure to focus the eye just right.

The other type of bifocal lens works in a completely different way. In fact, it may work two ways. First, instead of focusing all the light entering the eye to one place, because of its shape, it creates a gradual change in where the light is focused. This is helpful for near vision because it focuses near and far with a smoother transition. Also, this lens may actually move inside the eye in some patients. This causes the lenses to focus differently depending on what an individual wants to observe.

Currently, this is the lens I am recommending if someone wants one of these types of lenses. It is important to understand that all these lenses do some splitting of the light that comes into the eye. That means that there is some decrease in the quality of vision for both near and far.

My own opinion is that this approach to restoring both near and far vision in each eye remains the best deal as far as tradeoffs go. There seems to be less loss in near and far vision when they are split by this lens.

When discussing bifocal intraocular lenses, it is important to remember that there is some unpredictability to an individual's vision without glasses after cataract surgery. Astigmatism, measurement problems, and movement of the artificial lens inside the eye from natural healing processes can all influence the eventual vision without glasses. When I am planning multifocal lens surgeries, I tell the patients that they will probably need a second refractive procedure to get their eyes focused just right. For me that means LASIK. Often, incisions can be made during surgery that can reduce astigmatism. If they work, that's great. Usually I prefer the LASIK procedure to correct remaining astigmatism, nearsightedness, or farsightedness because it is so much more accurate and stable than other treatments.

Once a bifocal type of lens is implanted inside the eye, the only way to change it is another surgery. Unfortunately, the only way to know if someone will like this lens is to do the surgery. Then, after the surgery, if a person decides he doesn't like this division between near and far, the only way to fix the problem is to remove the bifocal lens and replace it with a different type of lens.

Each time eye surgery is done, we take risks. Yes, the risks are very small. But most eye doctors and patients would prefer to operate only once. So it is important to remember that if we decide to implant a bifocal intraocular lens, we may end up doing three surgeries. First is the standard cataract surgery using a bifocal lens inside the eye, then LASIK may have to be done to improve vision without glasses. Finally, we may have to remove the bifocal intraocular lens and replace it with a single focus intraocular lens if someone cannot tolerate this approach.

Astigmatism-Correcting Intraocular Lenses and Astigmatic Keratotomy

Once again, astigmatism is caused by an irregular focus by the focusing portions of the eye. In most people, this is caused by the cornea.

If the cornea isn't a perfect dome, it doesn't focus perfectly. The irregularity in the shape of this dome causes an irregular focus called astigmatism.

This can be corrected during cataract surgery with AK (astigmatic keratotomy) or with a special intraocular lens.

This technology is new at the time of this edition. However, it seems very promising, because once in place, intraocular lenses tend to remain tightly fixed in position. If someone is going to have surgery anyway, the idea of reducing astigmatism is a good one. Astigmatism can be a problem for people wearing glasses or contact lenses. Astigmatism causes distorted vision. The glasses for astigmatism cause a type of distortion of their own! Contact lenses for astigmatism have their own group of problems. They can be painful and generally difficult to use.

Commonly cataract surgery is combined with additional procedures to remove preexisting astigmatism. Incisions can be made at the time of cataract surgery to reduce astigmatism. This is called astigmatic keratotomy.

The trouble is that this approach is much less precise than the standard LASIK type of procedure. However, because it rarely causes problems, it is commonly performed. The idea here is that these astigmatism-reducing procedures may not work perfectly. But they usually improve vision without glasses, and they almost never cause problems. So there is little risk and some benefit. If I had astigmatism and were facing cataract surgery, I might have this procedure done, knowing I might not see perfectly without glasses. But I would expect to see better without them than I would otherwise.

Cataract Surgery

Part of the great honor of being an ophthalmologist is that we can reverse the aging process. Routinely I get to take a blind person with cataracts and give them pretty good distance vision without glasses. This is a profound event for both patient and doctor.

One of the many difficult parts of medical practice is managing the unrelenting decline of our elderly patients. When it comes to the eyes, this is not the usual case. My patients are generally surprised when I refer to cataract surgery as a happy event. But it is! Usually there is no pain. The quality of vision after recovery is commonly better than it has ever been!

In general, cataract surgery is 97% successful. This means 97% of surgeries result in excellent vision (with glasses) without problems of any kind. Usually the sedation and local anesthetic are quite effective. People usually don't remember the surgery. Patients, in general, suffer little or no pain, either during surgery or afterwards.

What will it be like after surgery?

The power of someone's glasses after cataract surgery almost always changes. The intraocular lens placed inside the eye has focusing power. This is customized to the each individual's eye, meaning that if someone needs powerful glasses before surgery, afterwards the glasses are usually not needed.

Cataract surgery can increase or decrease astigmatism. However, with modern cataract surgery, there is usually no significant effect on astigmatism. The trouble is, if you already have astigmatism, it will commonly limit your vision without glasses after surgery.

Will the cataract come back? Well, there is about a 20% chance of clouding of the natural container that holds the lens in place. If this happens enough to restrict vision, a laser can be used to permanently remove the cloudy area. This is called YAG laser capsulotomy. In this procedure, there is no pain. You don't have to change clothes, get an IV, or go into an operating room. It takes only a few minutes, and vision usually improves the same day. Of course, there are risks to everything, but complications of this procedure are very rare.

Pretreatment

Currently we like to give people Motrin-like drops (non-steroidal anti-inflammatory medications) before surgery. This improves the chance of better vision after surgery. These soothing drops reduce irritation and swelling. When any part of your body is swollen, it doesn't work well, and this also applies to the eye. We ask our patients to take this type of drop four times a day for at least two days before surgery. To reduce the chance of infection, we will sometimes ask patients to wash their eyelashes with special soaps before surgery. Germs are normally present here. By cleaning them away, fewer will be able to invade the eye during surgery. Antibiotic pills or eye drops before surgery may help prevent infection.

Story

By John Anthony Marin

I was born with my mother's eyes. Not good. But since I was raised in a wonderful middle-class Whittier household filled with a lot of love and opportunities, I never groused about my poor eyesight. Poetically, I got my first pair of glasses at age five at a place called "Superior Optical," which was directly across the street from Dr. May's current office. I still remember walking out of that office with my mom with a "Gee whiz!" outlook on life. That was forty-eight years ago. Over the course of those forty-eight years, my vision (I think it's called "myopia") got worse and my glasses got thicker and thicker. I still didn't grouse – it was just my lot in life.

However, for the last couple of years, my vision has gotten really bad. What really got my attention was when I went to buy another pair of glasses prior to an unexpected business trip to China. I was told that something else was going on and that corrective lenses were no longer a solution. I had no choice but to make the trip. Sure, I did my job, but I knew I'd have to address the issue when I got home.

I've had indirect contact with Dr. May (for brevity's sake, now referred to as either "Bill" or "MW" for Miracle Worker) because both my wife and my mother have been patients. When I returned from China, I shared my dilemma with my mother. She suggested that I make an appointment with MW. At first I resisted. After all, I've been a "manly man" my entire life and didn't require his or anybody else's help, for that matter. Then reality set in: I'm in sales. My job compels me to meet with new customers, and that compels me to find their offices. One day, shortly after my return from China, I found myself somewhere in the Chino area. I had to pull over, park my car, and walk to the end of the street to read the street sign. It was at that moment that I decided to make an appointment with MW. I called my mom, and she made the appointment. Mind you, I have always found the medical environment repugnant. Who wouldn't? After all, if you're in a doctor's office, something stinks in Denmark. But I allowed my mother to drag me, like a condemned man, to MW's office.

Our first meeting was so very, very cool. I had gone there to discuss laser surgery, but, after his examination, he told me that I had cataracts and they had to be taken care of. Idiot that I am, I then asked him if, after taking care of the cataracts, I would then be a candidate for laser correction. That's when he told me about the procedure that would correct my vision at the same time that he removed my cataracts!

Oh, and it got even better than that. The laser procedure is elective cosmetic surgery and not covered by my medical plan. Cataract surgery is a medical procedure and covered by my medical plan. MW and I scheduled the surgery on my left eye for January 3, 2007. I left his office on Cloud 8. I stepped up to Cloud 9 on Thursday, January 4. I COULD SEE! Darn it, for the first time in my life I could see this beautiful world without five pounds of glass perched on the bridge of my nose. I saw this world as I had never seen it before, and I wept. I wept all the way home. I pointed at street signs, and I wept. I pointed at the fine print on billboards, and I wept. I read the newspaper, and I wept. I received my co-payment bills in the mail and wept when I read them, too. I will take a moment out of every day for the rest of my life and give thanks for this miracle.

MW operated on my right eye yesterday, April 4. I'm writing this on the afternoon of April 5. After having my bandages removed this morning, I told MW that "this miracle comes in stereo."

~~~

Football, basketball, soccer, hockey – they are all sports. Indeed, honorable, competitive pursuits. But to me, baseball is not a sport. Baseball is a religion, and Dodgers Stadium is my place of worship. I've been going to my church since I was a little kid, but for the last couple of years, I couldn't see the game. Certainly, reading the scoreboard was out of the question, but it got even worse than that. I would hear "the crack of the bat," but I couldn't see where the ball went. I'd have to look at where the rest of the congregation had turned their heads.

On Monday, April 9, I will be going to Opening Day at Dodgers Stadium. I will be bringing my mother because, well, thanks to her, I met MW. I'm looking forward to walking into Dodgers Stadium with my new eyes. I know that I'll stand there for a moment and weep. Thanks to MW, I'll probably be able to see the stitches on the baseball. By the way, there are 108 stitches on a baseball, the same number as there are beads on a rosary. Another reason that God compels us to worship baseball. *Old Testament, Book of Genesis, Chapter One, Verse*

One: "In the big inning . . ."

Self-esteem is another huge benefit. When MW initially told me that he could fix my eyes and I could throw my glasses away, I embarked on a makeover plan. I'm assuming that if you're reading this, you, too, have spent most of your life burdened with poor eyesight—ridiculed as a kid, limited sports/physical participation, feeling like a geek. And like everyone else, I had all of this other garbage goin' on in my life that lowered my self-esteem to basement level. However, in concert with MW's procedure, I joined a diet plan (I do not want to endorse any plan, but it kinda rhymes with "The Washers"). At this writing, I've lost 44 pounds, and my new appearance has made me the butt of some flattering jokes, such as, "Where's John Marin? You know, the fat guy with the thick glasses?" MW helped me back on the path to self-respect. Given more time, I could (and probably will) go on *ad nauseum* about Dr. May, a.k.a. MW. I just wanted to get my initial interview thoughts on paper.

Dr. May's Comments about John Marin

Vision is a wonderful thing. Improving someone's vision is an honor. It transcends the routine problems of life. It is inspiring to care for this wonderful man.

Yes, I am a miracle worker and a shameless self-promoter. However, any ophthalmologist around the world can perform this miracle. This wonderful outcome is the standard result of cataract surgery. It is a tribute to the cooperation between the companies who manufacture these lenses and the many thousands of ophthalmologists who developed this surgery.

John could have gone to a place where they only do LASIK. Sometimes these businesses are structured so that the patient only sees the doctor when arriving at the laser. If a person goes to a "LASIK factory" and talks to people who are non-doctors, bonus money may influence the discussion about whether or not to have LASIK.

LASIK would have partially improved his vision. But to get to full vision, he would have needed cataract surgery. He had only one surgery, and it fixed both cataracts and nearsightedness. I am a very bad businessman. I could have operated twice! Instead, one surgery fixed both problems. When will I learn?

My Comments about Cataract Surgery

If you live long enough, you will eventually have cataract

surgery. Don't worry – it's normal! It is relatively safe compared to other surgeries. The way I do it either causes no pain at all or only a mild discomfort that can be treated with just Tylenol®. If you have functional problems, like trouble driving or reading even while wearing glasses, you should have this surgery. Cataracts either get worse or stay the same. They will not improve.

Most people love the result. Color vision improves. Vision without glasses usually improves. The potential for serious problems does exist, but the chance of blindness from cataract surgery is around one in one thousand. Ninety-seven percent of people have no problems of any kind!

Chapter 6

Glaucoma

Glaucoma is a disease that causes permanent, untreatable blindness. This means absolutely no vision. Completely black. Nothing. It is permanent. No cure. So we eye doctors take this disease very seriously. So much so that we are constantly looking for people at risk for this disease. And that's a lot of people. Some estimates are as high as 5% of the population. We want to find them early and treat them before they start going blind. We look hard for these people because once this loss develops, it is permanent. So we try to find people at risk. We watch them carefully. We want to find it before they know about it and treat it so they never notice any visual loss. Unfortunately, sometimes these people suffer high pressure and visual loss no matter how hard we try to control their glaucoma.

Even these people are better off if they are found early.

In the standard form of glaucoma, there is a slow, progressive visual loss caused by increased pressure inside the eye. This shouldn't be confused with blood pressure. The eye has its own pressure. It is a closed system that makes and drains fluid. The strange thing about the eye is that it continues to make fluid at a constant rate. If there is a drainage problem, the eye continues to produce the same amount of fluid. So the pressure goes up. This increase in pressure causes gradual damage to the optic nerve. This is the nerve that carries vision. Once this nerve is gone, all the vision is gone.

In general, to have glaucoma, a person must have three things. The first is increased intraocular pressure. Usually we say that normal pressure inside the eye is less than or equal to 20. But some people need to have a pressure lower than 20. The second is loss of side vision. This is also known as visual field loss. The third is an increased "cup to disc ratio." This is a rather technical term meaning an abnormal appearance of the optic nerve when an eye doctor examines your eye. The thing is, someone could have any one of these three without having glaucoma, so individualized evaluation by a competent eye doctor is a must.

Types of Glaucoma

Acute and Chronic

Actually, there are many different types of glaucoma. However, generally there are two broad categories: acute and chronic.

Acute glaucoma is much more dramatic, but it is also quite rare in the U.S. If you are having an attack of acute glaucoma, you will notice sudden severe loss of vision and severe pain in one eye. If this happens, go straight to the emergency room. Attacks of glaucoma can cause blindness within a day. They are more common in older people, farsighted people, and people of Chinese ancestry. The basic idea here is that the passage of the fluid the eye makes gets blocked. It can't get to the drain, and the eye keeps making more fluid because it can't tell it has enough. These eyes tend to be smaller than normal. It is as if the furniture is normal size but the room is smaller, so it is hard to move around. If the furniture is arranged in a particular way in this small room, you can't walk across.

The good news is that an alternate pathway can be created with a laser. No surgery is necessary. After one of these alternate paths has been created, it is theoretically impossible to have an attack of glaucoma. It is a simple, easy, and relatively safe procedure.

The best situation when people have these small eyes is to identify them before they have attacks of glaucoma. When they come into my office, I can tell if they are at risk during their examination. The problem comes when, during a routine eye examination, I tell them they are at risk for attacks of acute glaucoma. They usually look at me with a puzzled look and say, "I am just here for a routine eye exam and glasses." I guess no one wants to hear that they have a significant problem. Usually these people are coming to me for the first time. Otherwise, I would have already identified and treated them. So they don't know me, and suddenly I am telling them they need treatment. No one else has been saying things like this at their other exams. Of course, their eyes have been constantly changing, and they have had to buy a thousand dollars worth of new glasses every year. Now I am saying that they need a procedure. Not only that, but I tell them that they don't need new glasses!

They look at me with a familiar suspicious look. I usually think to myself, *Why don't I just say what they expect to hear? I could make more money. I wouldn't have to spend time explaining why I'm different from their previous eye doctors. Oh well, I am cursed with excellence!* If only my mother and my teachers at USC had not expected so much of me. This is usually when I suggest a second opinion. How can these people know the truth without asking another authority?

When people with attacks of glaucoma come into the emergency room complaining of severe pain and visual loss, their attack can usually be controlled with medications. Later, they can have the laser treatment we talked about earlier. It is called laser peripheral iridotomy. This means a tiny opening is made in the far periphery of the iris (near the white part of the eye). Why do we do this? The blockage of flow inside the eye occurs at the pupil. That is the dark circle in the middle of the iris. Fluid can't flow from the back to the front of the eye where it drains.

When we open a very tiny hole in the outer iris, this creates an alternate way for fluid to flow. We love alternate routes in traffic-filled Los Angeles. Angle-closure glaucoma is like a completely blocked freeway with no way off. The laser treatment for this is like an off-ramp to another parallel freeway. Even if you don't yet have traffic jams, it is nice to construct an off-ramp to another route.

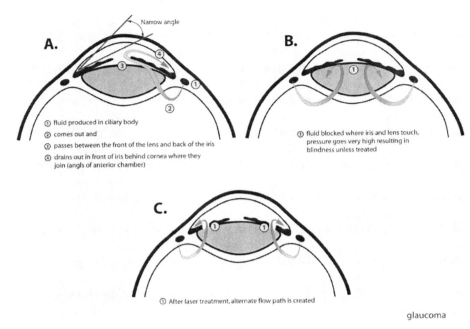

A.
Narrow angle

① fluid produced in ciliary body
② comes out and
③ passes between the front of the lens and back of the iris
④ drains out in front of iris behind cornea where they join (angls of anterior chamber)

B.
① fluid blocked where iris and lens touch, pressure goes very high resulting in blindness unless treated

C.
① After laser treatment, alternate flow path is created

glaucoma

The other broad category of glaucoma is called chronic open angle. In this type of glaucoma, the pressure in the eye is elevated above 20 millimeters of mercury (this is the standard unit of pressure measurement). There is damage to the optic nerve and side vision loss. These people usually take years to go blind. The trouble is, it sneaks up on you. Some eye doctors call it "the silent thief of sight." You can have it for years and not know! During this time, the side vision loss is so slow you don't notice it until you look at something out of one eye and notice you can only see half of it. At this point, that part of your vision is gone. Nothing can bring it back.

We want to find glaucoma before you lose that half. That is why we almost always check the eye's pressure. No, I don't mean that horrible puff of air. We never use that in my office. That machine is a pretty reliable test the first time you do it to someone. The puff of air is a surprise! And it hurts. If you can keep the patient from running out of the room and talk him into letting you do it on his second eye, he is usually squeezing his eyes so much that there is a falsely high pressure reading. In my office we use much more gentle means. There is no pain.

The process of discovering if someone has glaucoma is done in steps. Usually, either high pressure or optic nerve changes are noticed on routine exams. These people come into my office wanting to know right away if they have glaucoma. I usually can't answer this on the first visit because I don't have a visual field test result. When I say this, people usually close one eye and start to wave their hands on the side. Then I stop to explain that it is more complex than that. You see, what we are talking about early in glaucoma isn't actually blackness. It is reduced sensitivity to dim lights to the side. The eye is much more sensitive to light in the center of vision.

You can see a campfire miles away from an airplane at thirty thousand feet if you are looking straight at it. But if you look a little to the side, the light disappears. This is a demonstration of the decreasing sensitivity to light as it comes farther from the side. A visual field test checks your sensitivity to very dim lights off to the side. If you have less sensitivity than normal, you can see your hand waving but not very dim lights. This is characteristic of early glaucoma.

We want to find this disease when you still don't know you have side vision changes. We want to freeze it here, for at this point you don't notice any visual loss. You are okay. Your best chance to stay that way is to work with an ophthalmologist.

The second part of checking for glaucoma is looking at the optic nerve. Once again, this is the nerve that carries the sight, and it's actually part of the brain. It is the only part of the brain that can be seen without surgery. Usually, to see this nerve well, your eyes have to be dilated. Your eye doctor will put obnoxious stinging drops in your eyes. After a while, these will open your pupils so we can look inside. We use special microscopes and magnifying lenses to get a really good look at this tiny nerve. A person with glaucoma will have less of this nerve that carries sight. Because that part is in the middle of this nerve when it is lost, a cuplike depression (like a pot hole in a road) forms in the center. And like a pothole that is not repaired, it gets bigger and deeper if the glaucoma is not controlled.

As progressive nerve damage develops, sensitivity to dim lights on the side decreases. Eventually these areas can't see anything. If eye pressure is left uncontrolled, these black areas very slowly move to the center of vision. Then people notice them. Again, at this point all those black areas are permanent.

Once we identify someone with glaucoma, we want to get the pressure below 20 millimeters of mercury. That is our usual "target pressure." This target could change depending on your individual response to treatment. Some people require pressures well below 20. When people ask me about how we can control pressure, I say, "Drops, pills, laser, and surgery." We usually start with drops.

We have some great eye drop glaucoma medications these days. A very popular type of treatment is "prostaglandin analogs." The trade names of these three drugs are Xalatan®, Lumigan®, and Travatan®. We like these drugs because they are really good at lowering pressure and they only have to be used once a day. Their potential side effects are not serious as far as health goes. The main problem with these drops is chronic redness and darker pigmentation of the skin around the eyes. And yes, these drops can cause blue eyes to turn brown. It is rare, but it can happen. They can also cause eyelashes to become thicker and longer. My female patients are usually happy about this.

Side Effects of Drugs

A better way to discuss side effects is to describe them as potential side effects. They probably won't happen! When I innocently answer (in my medical mode) what the side effects of a drug are, I am thinking like a doctor. That means I am remembering potential problems and reciting a list. I am expecting to try it and see how it goes. When a patient responds, "Oh no, I don't want that," I stop and explain that a drug side effect is merely a possibility. It probably will not happen. If you say to your doctor you don't want to treat your glaucoma because of the potential side effects of drops, you are saying you would rather go completely and permanently blind than take the small risk of these rare side effects. The way it works in medicine is that we try various treatments while looking for side effects and benefits. Of course, if we know someone is allergic to a drug or if we know it doesn't work for them, we don't try it. Treatment decisions about glaucoma should be made by a qualified ophthalmologist. Find a good one. Work with your doctor. Adjustments will be made according to your individual responses to specific medicines.

Treatment Problems/Compliance

The trouble is that some people need more than one type of eye drop to treat their glaucoma. This may mean one drop once a day. Other treatments could be twice a day. Still others can be used three or four times a day. It is possible for someone to need to take all these drops at all these different times each day! Long-term studies show that it is common for people on lots of different drops to progressively lose their vision even though they have good pressure control when they see their eye doctor. Why this happens is controversial. I think it is partly because many people are just not capable of using lots of different drops at the correct times every day of their lives. Of course they make sure to use the drops like they are supposed to just before they come in for their appointments. This way everything seems fine during the doctor visit. Usually that's only twice a year!

When I was in college I did an independent study project on compliance with medication prescriptions. These studies involved counting pills that were actually left in a bottle and comparing to the number that should be there. They discovered repeatedly that about 1/3 of patients used all their pills. About 1/3 of patients used some of their pills. Finally, 1/3 of patients used none of their pills! So some of us think that the fewer drops we ask our patients to take, the more likely they are to actually use the medications correctly. They then are less likely to lose their vision.

This is why we love those once-a-day drops. You can just use them at night before going to bed. Many studies show that the less we ask you to do, the more likely you are to do it. This is one of my personal basic medical principles.

There is a relatively new laser treatment that allows us to reduce or eliminate the use of drops. From my point of view, laser treatment is great. I think it is a lot better for me to do something one time a year to control someone's glaucoma than having them put drops in their eyes every day for the rest of their lives. My patients commonly complain that they are on many different expensive medications. They love it when they don't need some or all of the glaucoma medications after laser.

So how do these treatments work? As you know, the eye both makes and drains fluid. This drain is an interesting thing.

First, there is a filter-like structure called the trabecular meshwork. This structure first filters the fluid the eye makes. "Why does it do this?" you might ask. Well, particles naturally get inside the eyes. Things like blood and pigment need to be removed when they get in there. There are cells inside the drain of the eye called macrophages. These are essentially drain-cleaning cells. Scanning laser trabeculoplasty (SLT) is a laser treatment that activates these cells. Not only does it make them multiply, it makes them work harder to clean the drain. Because there are more of them and they are working harder, the drain is more open and fluid drains better. This is why pressure goes down.

Story of Lenore Stein

By Marina Marin

About seven years ago when LS began to see Dr. May, he put her on eye drops and pills. After a period of time on these drops, she started suffering side effects. They included red eyes and intense headaches. It was discovered that she was allergic to every drop and pill for glaucoma.

Everything was done to work around the fact that she was allergic to all glaucoma medications. "It was a step-by-step procedure and frightening at times," says Stein, who had many surgeries done on both eyes.

She had laser twice on her right eye, three times on the left eye, two glaucoma surgeries in the right eye, and one in the left.

"I woke up one morning and I couldn't see in my right eye because glaucoma had started pretty bad," she said.

After the first glaucoma surgery, she recovered well. "But the pressure didn't go down, and I had to return for another surgery," said Stein, who approached every surgery optimistically.

Now she is able to keep a balanced pressure of 15 in both eyes. "Dr. May has been able to preserve my eyesight. His aggressive approach to save my vision was crucial," said Stein.

It is estimated that over 3 million Americans have glaucoma. Because this condition does not cause symptoms in its early stages, people often don't know they have it.

This story is a good example of how many different ways we have to treat glaucoma. When patients ask how we treat this disease, the answer is, "Drops, pills, laser, and surgery."

Recommendations

Be honest with yourself about how regularly you take your

drops. If you miss drops, your pressure may go up. This causes a little bit of permanent visual loss, and it builds up. Every time you miss a drop, you lose some vision. It will never come back. Blindness from glaucoma is common even in people who see an eye doctor. Tell your eye doctor if you are taking too many drops at too many different times of the day and you just can't keep track. Have surgery or laser if you can't take your drops exactly as prescribed.

If your father or mother has had glaucoma, get your eyes checked by an ophthalmologist at least once a year. If you find this problem early and take care of it correctly, you will give yourself the best possible chance of not losing your vision. If you get glaucoma and don't take care of it correctly, you will go completely blind.

Chapter 7

Glasses

Understanding Your Outer Lens

Myopia (Nearsightedness)

Remember that the eye is like a camera. The front is like a lens, and the back is like film. Myopia happens when the lens system focuses light into the middle of the eye in front of the retina instead of onto it. Then light spreads out so that when it reaches the retina, it is seen as a blur. These people can see near but not far, so they are nearsighted.

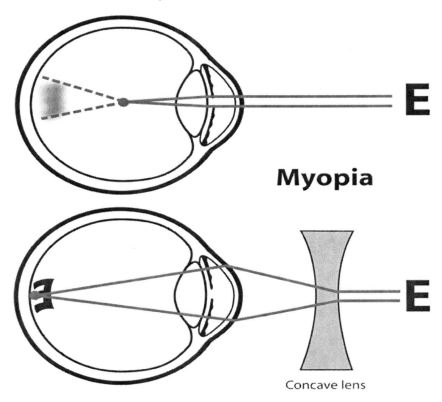

Myopia

Concave lens

Myopia means light is focused in front of the retina (film-like part of the eye). When it arrives at the film it is out of focus. The front of the eye bends light too much and the light comes into focus before it should. If something is very close, the light is spreading out when it arrives at the focusing part of the eye. But the front of the eye still bends the light coming from an object the same way. Images up close are therefore in focus because their spreading light rays are bent so much that they come into focus on the back of the eye. Glasses for myopia work the same way. They cause light to diverge when it hits the eye. That way, when the front of the eye bends this light, it is still in focus.

Glasses for myopia change the focus onto the retina. They essentially diverge light or spread it out. This is the opposite of what we usually think of a lens doing. Normally a lens takes parallel rays of light and brings them together at one point. The more powerful a lens is, the more it bends light and the closer it focuses light to the lens. We use this kind of lens (called a converging lens) to treat farsightedness.

At the age of nine, I distinctly remember asking my mother if she could see a sign in the distance that I could not. She took me to an eye doctor where we discovered that I was nearsighted. As we left, she was very angry with me because she thought that I had caused this nearsightedness by sitting too close to the TV, reading at night, and reading in the car. Later, as I went through my ophthalmology training, I kept expecting to learn why sitting too close to the TV, reading in the dark, and reading in the car caused myopia. It never happened. These things don't cause nearsightedness or any other problem. I sat too close to the TV because I couldn't see unless I did. I read at night and in the car because I loved to read. None of that caused any problems. My father was nearsighted, and I inherited my need for glasses!

After becoming a board-certified ophthalmologist, I

confronted my mother about this. When I told her that sitting too close to the TV, reading in the dark, and reading in the car don't cause any eye problems, her response was, "You don't know."

Later, I had children. Their first-grade teacher invited me to give a talk about the eye and how it works. They brought in about a hundred children to hear me speak. After my lecture, a small boy in the front row asked me, "Is it true that reading in the dark, sitting too close to the TV, and reading in the car are bad for your eyes?" I looked down at him and thought for a while. Then I said, "You do what your mother tells you!"

Hyperopia (Farsightedness)

In myopia, the front of the eye is too powerful. It brings light into focus before it needs to.

In hyperopia, or farsightedness, light is brought into focus too late. Or another way of saying it is that the front of the eye is not powerful enough. The light entering the eye never comes to a point of focus. So it also is seen as a blur.

If the hyperopia is not too bad, then the lens inside the eye can make a focusing effort and bring light into focus by changing its shape from a muscular contraction. In this case, there is not enough focusing power left to see near. These people can see far away and are thus farsighted.

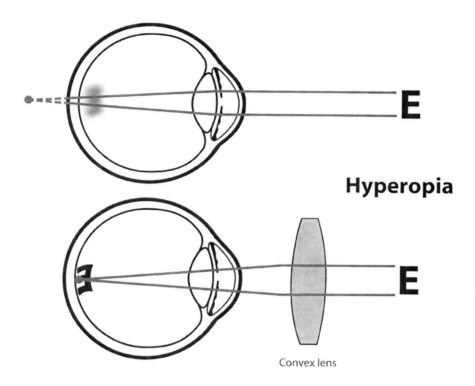

Hyperopia

Convex lens

In hyperopia, the eye doesn't have enough light-bending power. The light never comes into focus before it hits the film-like part in the back of the eye. Lenses for hyperopia converge light before it gets to the eye. They help the eye bend the light more so it can come into focus on the film-like part of the eye.

In severe farsightedness, the lens cannot focus light enough to make a person see near or far. These people must use glasses or contact lenses to see anything.

In mild farsightedness, only a small part of the lens's power is used to see distance. These people are said to have "latent hyperopia." They need reading glasses before their friends of the same age. This happens because part of the lens's focusing power is always used to see far. That means less power is left for near vision. When the natural process causing near vision problems happens, less focusing power is available as a natural aging change. The age where near vision problems develop happens earlier as the lens loses all of its focusing power. These people have been using this power to see distance, so they eventually suffer decreased vision even in the distance.

Astigmatism

Astigmatism is a situation where the curve of the cornea is not like a perfect dome. A sphere cut in half is a perfect dome shape. Clear glass shaped like this will bring light into focus essentially at one place. If this glass was flexible and you pulled opposite edges of this shape apart, you would create a distorted shape with different curves. Each curve focuses light differently. So light would be focused by this shape in different places. It would not be focused to a single point. This is astigmatism. There is no one point of focus; instead, there is a blur.

Astigmatism

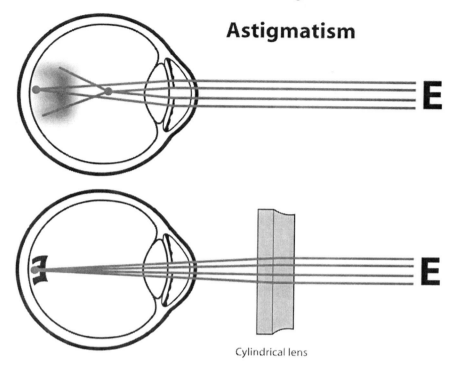

Cylindrical lens

If the cornea has more than one curve, it will focus light in different places according to how much a certain part is curved. Light must be focused in just one place to make an image that can be seen by the brain. Astigmatism-correcting lenses focus only along one line across the cornea. They move the focusing points together by equalizing the focusing power (light bending) around the whole cornea. That way, light can come onto focus in one place and be seen by the brain.

Presbyopia

"Trouble reading when you are old like I am."

The eye normally needs to focus both far away and close up.

That is why it has two lenses.

The cornea is a rigid lens. It focuses light with the same power all the time. The natural or crystalline lens changes its focusing power to see near. It does this when a muscle inside the eye contracts and changes the lens shape. So when a normal eye is relaxed, it is focused in the distance. Anything closer than twenty feet involves a focusing effort by this lens and muscle.

When people get to around forty, they notice trouble focusing near. They come into my office saying that all at once they developed this problem. But this is a problem that has been developing their whole life. Babies see well at the tip of their nose. Then the nearest point a person can see gradually moves away from the face each year of life. This is because the lens gradually becomes less flexible. There is no weakness involved; the muscle pulling on the lens is still just as strong. The lens just doesn't change shape as well and therefore cannot focus on objects as close as before.

When I was a medical student, I was amazed when I used a scale that exactly correlated my focusing ability with my age of 25. Later, I can remember being fascinated by how close my daughters held things to their faces when they were toddlers. At that age, when they showed me something they wanted me to see really well, they would push it right up to my nose. They were expecting that I could see as well as they could up close. Of course, at age 38 I had to move my head back to see near objects well. But they would hold interesting things almost to their nose. Later, as they grew older they would hold these objects of interest gradually farther and farther away. This was a completely unconscious change. They simply were holding things as near as they could while still keeping them in focus.

A common misconception is that using reading glasses will make your eyes weaker. They don't. In fact, after the age of nine, glasses have no physical impact on your eyes. People notice that the power of their reading glasses gets stronger with time. They feel bad for relying on this crutch and becoming weaker. They come in guiltily admitting that their problem with near vision was caused by their use of "cheaters." But it wasn't! The increase in power for near glasses happens in everyone. There is no difference in how fast it increases between people who read with near glasses and those who don't.

This situation provides a great opportunity for a doctor like me. We physicians are always telling people to do something they don't want to do. Or we're telling them not to do something they want to do. In fact, we learn in medical school,

"If it feels good or tastes good, don't do it." In this case, I get to give permission to go ahead and do what you want. I love it. I usually take a break from my busy day and revel in permission-giving. "Go ahead," I tell them. "Do whatever you want. Wear as many different glasses as you want for as long as you want. Wear your friend's glasses. Wear your mother's glasses. Go to the drug store and buy lots of different power glasses and use them all. It doesn't matter. The worst that could happen is that you will get a headache. But that will go away when you take them off."

Why I Can't See Close after Forty without Glasses

Presbyopia

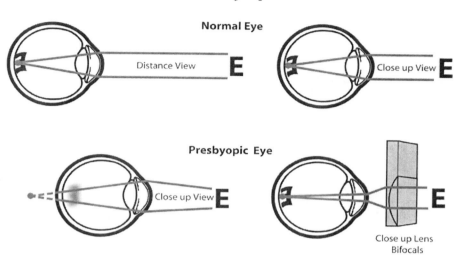

The normal eye bends the incoming light so that it comes into focus at a single point on the back of the eye. This causes the retina at the back of the eye to make an image that can be seen by the brain. How much the eye has to bend the light increases as an image comes closer. The eye increases its ability to focus or bend light by using the ciliary muscle to change the shape of the lens inside the eye. Older people lose flexibility of their lens. To see near they need more light-bending power from reading glasses or a more powerful bending lens in the bottom of bifocals.

How Glasses Work

Glasses lenses are made of prisms put together a particular way. A prism is a piece of glass or plastic that gradually increases in thickness from one side to the other.

Parallel Light Rays

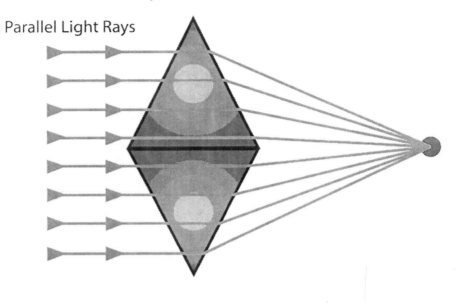

Converging Lens

This type of lens helps bring light together. It is useful when the eye cannot bend light enough. This includes both farsightedness and reading glasses for older people. These lenses are what people call "magnifiers."

Prisms bend light. They bend it towards the thicker side as it passes through clear material. Farsighted glasses are essentially two prisms stuck together at the thick ends (a converging lens). They bend light to the thick part of the two prisms. In this case, they bend light into the eye because the eye doesn't have enough power to bend the light by itself.

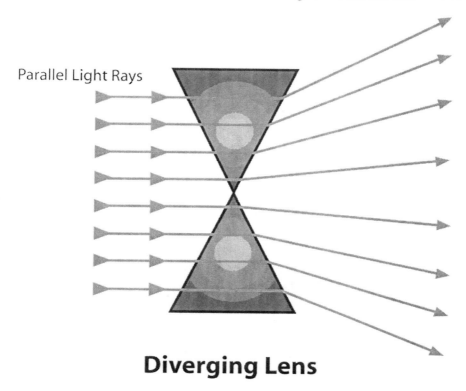

Parallel Light Rays

Diverging Lens

On the other hand, myopic glasses bend light away from the thick part of the prism. This is known as a diverging lens.

Diverging Lens for Nearsightedness

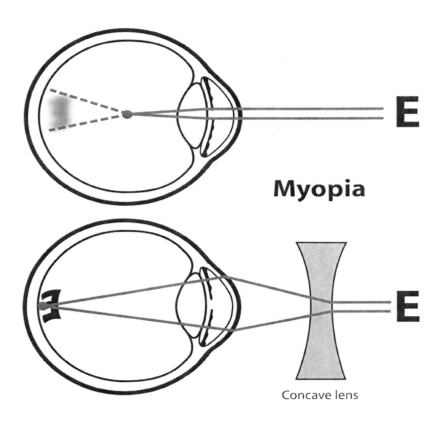

Myopia

Concave lens

When the focusing part of the eye is too powerful, a person becomes nearsighted. This is because light rays have to be spreading out to be in focus on the film-like portion of the eye (retina). Normally light rays are parallel when they hit the eye. These rays are brought into focus before they get to the retina. If the rays are diverging or spreading out before they come to the eye, the excessive focusing power of myopia brings the light into focus on the back of the eye. Near location and diverging lenses put nearsighted eyes into focus because these light rays are spreading out when they hit the eye.

These figures show lenses in two dimensions, that is, in cross section. In three dimensions, myopic glasses are shaped like a clear coin that is thinner in the center. Hyperopic lenses are shaped like a coin thicker in the center. Light is focused in the shape of a cone to one point. This happens in three dimensions so that light hitting any part of the lens focuses to the same single point.

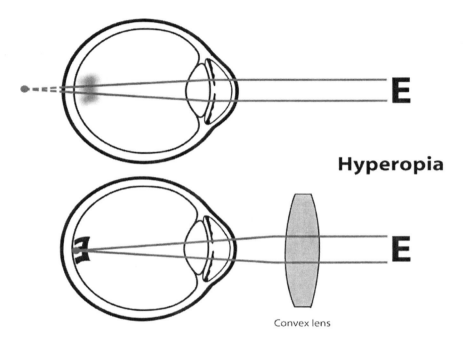

Hyperopia

Convex lens

Hyperopic lenses add increased bending power so that an eye that cannot bring light into focus can converge the light on the back of the eye.

Hyperopic lens

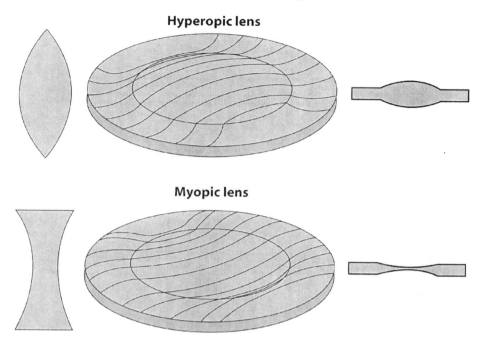

Myopic lens

Hyperopic or converging lenses are thicker in the middle and make your eyes look bigger when you wear them. Myopic lenses are thinner in the middle and make your eyes look smaller.

Astigmatism Lenses

Unlike myopic or hyperopic lenses, glasses for astigmatism really do work in two dimensions. They have an "axis." That means that if you draw a line through the middle of a circle from one side to the other, all the light hitting that line will be focused. Light hitting the other parts of the circle will not be focused.

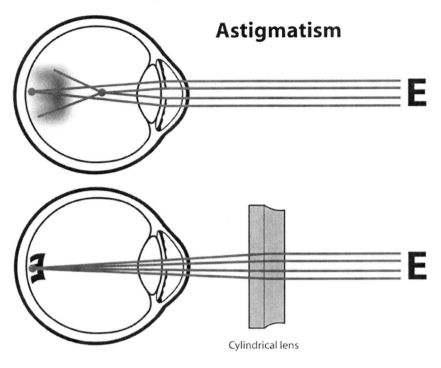

Astigmatism

Cylindrical lens

Light that hits the lens in a particular line gets the full power of the correcting lens. The lens bends the light the most along this line. If we were to shrink ourselves to the size of an ant and get onto a glass lens as it was being worn and travel in a circle around the center, we would notice that light hitting the "power axis" was focused the most. As we travel the circle, we would notice that light is focused gradually less and less until we get to the part one quarter of the circle away from where we started on the power axis. At this point (90 degrees away from the power axis) we would notice that light is actually not being focused at all! Then as we continue to travel our circle we would see that light is gradually focused more and more until we reach a point at the exact opposite end of the circle from our starting point (180 degrees away). At this location on the circle we would notice that light was focused exactly as much as where we started. Then as we continue to travel the circle we have an experience of déjà vu. "Wait a minute," we say, "we've been here before." The same identical thing happens as when we left the starting point. Power decreases to no focusing at 90 degrees and then increases again to the same peak power when we get back to the starting point. Hopefully we can get off the circle and do something more fun now.

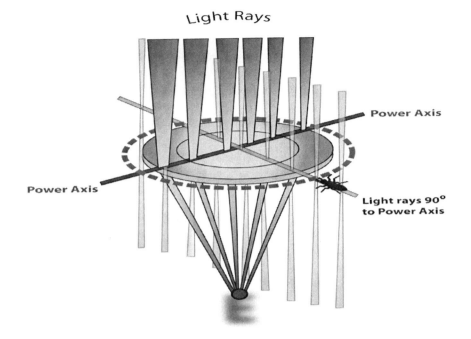

The trouble is, we are still shrinking. Now we hitch a ride on a piece of dust. As we are slowly floating away from the lens surface, we can see the surface of the eye below. We notice that the cornea is not a perfect dome. It looks like the surface of a clear American football. It has a shallow curve and a steeper curve. Suddenly we realize how it all works.

We notice that the shallower curve of the cornea is perfectly aligned with the power axis on the glasses lens. We realize that since shallower curves don't focus light as powerfully, the power axis of the glasses' lens adds just enough focusing help to match the more powerful steeper curve of the clear football surface.

Now how do we get back to our original size? I don't know; I'm just an ophthalmologist!

Myopia and Hyperopia Mixed with Astigmatism

To fix these two problems, glasses are made by putting two lenses together. The astigmatism lens and the myopia lens are essentially pressed together to make one lens that solves both problems.

Bifocals

Often people will have myopia or hyperopia mixed with astigmatism and will be over forty! These people also will need reading help. Glasses can be made by pressing yet another lens onto the glasses. But this one is on the lower half of the lens. With these, people can see far things over the top of the lens and near things through the lower part. Interestingly, this is done by pressing essentially the same lens you could get in a drug store onto the lower half. But these lenses have to be the same on both sides, or the near focus will be in different places.

Eye doctors have something called trial frames in their

offices. These are a way to show someone what it would be like to wear the glasses the eye doctor wants to give you. They have an adjustable frame with places to put three lenses in front of each other. The three slots are for three possible lenses. One is for farsightedness or nearsightedness. The other is for astigmatism. The third is to add another lens in front of these two to focus someone for near. In regular glasses, any combination of these can be put together.

Problems with Glasses

Remember that glasses are made of prisms. Prisms bend light. They have to be made into a particular shape to improve vision. If you put just any old prism in front of one eye, it will bend the light so that what the eye sees moves to a different place. The other eye without a prism still sees things in the real position. So this causes double vision.

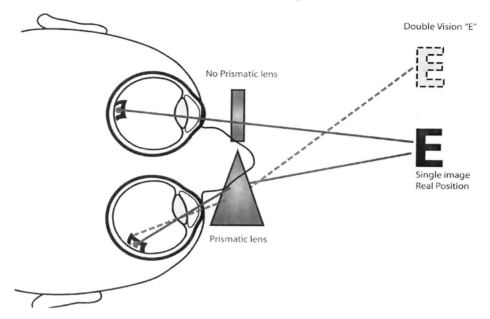

When glasses lenses are off center, it creates a prism effect. The thing you are looking at is moved to the side in one eye. The brain tries to move the image together by contracting the muscles that move the eye around. This causes a type of eye strain.

If the prism is not too powerful, you can use your eye muscles to force the image together. This is a type of "eye strain" and can cause headaches. When your eye muscles get tired from all this contraction, they stop making the effort to stay together, and then the image goes double again.

If you put the same prism in front of both eyes, images move the same amount. Then there is no double vision. No muscular effort is needed to bring the images together. Thus, there is no eye strain.

"Why are we talking about this?" you might ask. Glasses lenses have an optical center. The farther away from this center the eye looks, the more images are moved. If glasses are off-center, they can move the images even while looking straight ahead. The result is constant eye muscle effort. This can cause headaches and double vision whenever you wear the glasses. Think back to the analogy of a coin thicker or thinner at the center. This coin has to be centered on the middle of the eye. If its center is not lined up with the center of the eye, there will be a separation of images through a prism effect.

A person with very different power nearsighted or farsighted lenses has another problem. These lenses actually change the size of images. A lens for nearsightedness will make the image smaller. A lens for farsightedness will make the image larger. You can see this effect by looking at people wearing powerful glasses. If they are farsighted, their eyes will seem larger. The side of their head, seen through the glasses, will seem wider. If they are nearsighted, their eyes will seem smaller. The side of their head you can see through their glasses will seem caved in. When a person with very different power lenses looks through their glasses, they see the same difference.

One eye sees things larger than the other. Depending on how different these sizes are, a person may or may not be able to adapt.

I run into prism effects a lot after cataract surgery. If someone has a cataract and is very farsighted or nearsighted, I warn them that it will be hard to wear the glasses after the first cataract surgery. I tell them this will happen because I plan to do "too good of a job." After surgery they usually see quite well without glasses in the operated eye. The other eye still needs a thick lens to see. So when I give them glasses with essentially no power in one lens and their old thick lens in front of the other eye, two things happen. First, when they look straight ahead, everything will seem bigger on one side and smaller on the other. When they look to the side, they will see double because one eye will get a prism effect from a powerful lens. The other eye will see without any prism bending the light. The powerful lens will cause a false image separated from its true position in space. The eye that doesn't need a powerful lens will see the image where it actually exists in space. This separation of images will make the brain try to bring these images together.

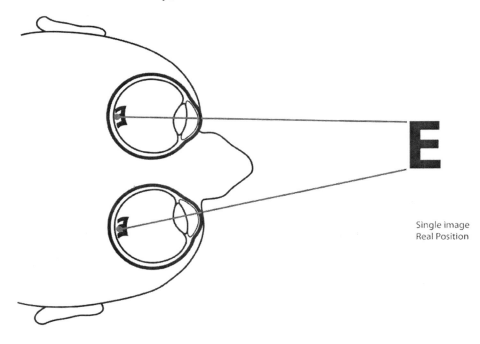

Single image
Real Position

Each eye sees one image. The brain automatically brings the eyes together so that the two images are superimposed. That way you see just one image.

Even if the glasses are made correctly, when a person looks away from the center of the lens, a separation of images will occur. This is because when looking to the side, the eye without any focusing power has no prism effect. The image is not moved. The eye with nearsighted or farsighted power has more and more separation of images the farther to the side one looks.

"What do I do if I am one of these people?" you might ask. Well, we could put a contact lens on one eye to equalize it with the other. Then we could use glasses. At this point people usually say, "Why not just use contact lenses on both eyes?" The answer is we could! Or we could do LASIK on one or both eyes (more on this in the refractive surgery chapter). At this point you might also ask, "Do contact lenses cause this same effect?" The answer is no. That is good news cosmetically. Contact lens wear for nearsighted people lets their eyes appear to be normal size and doesn't make the side of their heads seem indented. Farsighted people lose that abnormally large look to their eyes.

"Astigmatism lenses make things seem like they're in the wrong place."

Another problem with adjusting to glasses is caused by something every astigmatism lens causes. This is "spatial distortion." Astigmatism-correcting lenses make things seem like they are in the wrong place. How hard this makes it to adjust to a new pair of glasses depends on the individual, the amount of astigmatism power, and its direction. Spatial distortion creates a decision-making problem for eye doctors. Sometimes people come in with eyes that have developed a different type of astigmatism. With their current glasses, they don't see as well as they could with a new pair. If I change their glasses' power to the new type of astigmatism, they will see better on the eye chart. But there is a good chance they will get mad at me because things won't seem like they are in the correct location. Objects will appear distorted even though they see the 20/20 line on the eye chart. They will wonder why they spent $500 for a new pair of high-fashion glasses with all the coatings when everything they see is in the wrong place! What do I do in these situations? Now I will give them this chapter of my book. Hopefully I won't get into this type of mess without first warning them about these problems.

Over-Minus

One of the first mistakes a beginning eye doctor makes is to "over-minus" someone. This means to give someone more power than they need in their myopic (nearsighted) glasses. Prism effects make the muscles that move the eye constantly strain. In contrast, too much myopic power makes the muscle inside the eye that usually focuses for near vision constantly contract. This can cause headaches. When people put these glasses on, they see out of each eye but the eyes don't feel right.

When I was getting my final training in ophthalmology,

there were four of us in my class at USC. We were all nearsighted. Part of learning about checking someone for glasses was to check each other. We knew it wasn't correct to give someone too much nearsighted power in their glasses. But we discovered that unanimously we preferred too much power ourselves. We all thought this was strange. We used to joke about how we preferred the wrong power. Back then, when we were in our twenties, we had lots of focusing ability. Our lenses inside our eyes easily took on the strain. And we noticed we could see better! This is the usual response in a young person.

Thus, as a friendly obliging beginning eye doctor, I found myself knowingly over-minusing my young patients. It was what they wanted! It couldn't hurt them. The trouble was that they all came back complaining of headaches. So I stopped doing that. Now I give just enough power to see 20/20 in each eye. Too much in either or both eyes causes chronic headaches.

If someone has just a little extra nearsighted power in their glasses' lenses of an equal amount, they must use the focusing power of their natural lens to see at all. If they are in their twenties, they won't notice. If they are in their late thirties, they will have trouble reading earlier than they would otherwise. None of these problems sound too bad. The trouble usually happens when one eye is over-minused and the other is not. The eye with too much focusing power in the glasses (over-minused) always has to use the focusing power of the natural lens to see clearly. The one with the correct power doesn't need any focusing power from the lens inside the eye.

A very interesting thing about the visual system is that the focusing signal coming out of the brain is always equal to both eyes. So if one eye is not in focus because it needs more focusing power and the other eye is in focus when the focusing signal comes out of the brain, it affects both eyes. It puts the over-minused eye into focus. At the same time, this signal causes the eye that has the correct glasses lens to go blurry. This eye is focusing too much. The brain, meanwhile, gets confused. The clear vision it uses to determine how much focusing signal to send out is different in each eye. Patients wearing these glasses usually will not know what is wrong in this kind of detail. They will just say they're not right! They are correct, because the eyes can't see at the same time.

Base Curve Problems

When people complain about their glasses not being right and none of the things just mentioned are happening, I check the base curve. This means I'm trying to find out if the lenses in a particular pair of glasses have different curvatures on their backside from each other.

If they are different, the prism effect develops at a different rate. Remember that when lenses are the same, there is no prism effect to separate images. Both images are moved to the side the same amount. There is no muscular effort to bring them together. If the prism effect develops faster on one side, then images will be separated and "eye strain" will occur when muscles are used to bring the images together. This is how eye strain develops in glasses with unequal base curve.

Problems with Bifocals

Another area where people run into problems with their glasses is when they move into bifocals. If you wear glasses, getting bifocals is a normal part of life. We all resist this and other aging changes. Sometimes people start with one pair of glasses for reading and another for distance. This is fine. Since glasses have no physical effect on your eyes (after the age of nine), anything is okay. But eventually most people who wear glasses end up in bifocals. They often tell me they just got tired of changing glasses every time they wanted to read.

The trouble is that bifocals come with their own set of problems. The first is that darn line. Women almost never want a line in their glasses when they first get bifocals. They tell me that it makes them look old. I usually sigh at this point, thinking that I have to warn them about the problems associated with bifocals without a line. I am usually worried that they are going to be mad at me about their upcoming adjustment problem.

Why do I think they are going to have a problem with this kind of lens? Well, a progressive lens gets more powerful as you look farther down the lens. So there is not one lens power. People have to adjust to this progressive increase in lens power. They have to understand that the full power of the lens only exists at the very bottom of the lower lens. The advantage to these lenses is that they provide a range where things can be seen. In contrast, a classic bifocal lens focuses in one place. If you move the print closer or farther than a specific area, the words are out of focus.

When I am in public, I can tell from across the room which kind of bifocal someone has. If they pick up reading material and nod their head up and down to find the exact part of the lower lens that brings the print into focus, they are wearing a progressive bifocal. If they pick up a piece of written material and move it back and forth to find the best focusing distance, they are wearing a classic single focus bifocal.

As it is with so many things, there is a tradeoff with each of these lenses. The progressives provide a nice range of focus. You can see countertops and read a book up close with these. However, in return for that increased range, you give up some visual quality. Also, it can be difficult to adjust to tilting your head to get things into focus.

With single focus bifocals, the visual quality is higher, but focusing only occurs at one distance. These lenses are a better idea for people who have other visual problems that limit their vision. For example, people with mild visual loss from macular degeneration should have this kind of lens. They already are compromised visually. They can't afford the distortion from a progressive bifocal lens.

Another problem that people have with bifocals is their position. Once the bifocal begins, distance vision ends. So if this lower lens is placed too high, it disrupts distance vision. Also, it may be hard to adjust to dramatically reduced vision when you look down. People who are new to bifocals have to adjust to tilting their head down to see where they are walking. They can't just point their eyes down.

Each individual is different in terms of where they prefer their bifocal lens to start. This means that every bifocal is a trial and error effort. If we give someone a pair of bifocals, we know they may come back saying the bifocal is in the wrong place. The trouble for us is that they are always right! Even if we put the bifocal where most people like it, it may not be the preferred place for an individual. When this happens, we talk to the patients and guess where they might like their bifocal to begin. Everyone has his or her own individual preference for this. In general, we try to evaluate their old glasses and keep the new lens at the same position.

Bifocals and the Elderly

As I am writing this, I am actively caring for a lady who has fallen twice in the last two weeks. When I walked into the exam room this week, I found her sitting calmly in the exam chair with lots of bruising all over her face. She told me that she had fallen two times in two weeks – on her face! When I asked her if she had the new glasses I prescribed without the bifocal yet, she said no. You see, when she came in last week after falling on her face the first time, I advised her to get out of bifocals so she could see where she was walking without tilting her head down. She replied that she had not gotten out of bifocals because she thought the problem was with her balance and not her vision.

I sighed and told her that balance has three parts. The first is the vestibular system. This part of the inner ear works with the brain to maintain balance. Next is the ability to locate yourself in space. When your eyes are closed, you know where your body parts are. This ability is called proprioception. The location of these parts is important information for the brain to maintain balance and coordinate movements. The third part of balance is the use of visual information to coordinate movements. All three affect balance.

If someone is developing balance problems, it usually is not primarily a visual problem. But improving vision can make these people better. Replacing bifocals with single vision lenses allows older people to see the cracks in the sidewalk and the toys left on the floor by their grandchildren. Falling is a major health risk in older people, and breaking a hip is often the result. This then leads to significant disability and possibly death from complications related to impaired mobility. So if you are falling a lot, stop using bifocals!

The Glasses Scam

One of the problems with checking someone for glasses is that the result is a little different every time. If I wanted to sell as many glasses as possible without regard for my patient's benefit, I would change their glasses every time they came in. And of course I would sell them every coating I could. Then, of course, they could use a spare pair in case they lose the first. But don't forget sunglasses. That's a third pair. Of course, all glasses are a fashion statement. You wear them on your face every day, so the highest fashion is appropriate. That is why someone needs to spend at least $500 on each pair!

It is pretty common for someone to come into my office complaining that they spent $1,000 on a couple pairs of glasses and don't see any better. They commonly bring a bag full of ten pairs of glasses discussing what is good and bad about each one. When we check the power of the lenses in each one, all ten are about the same! They tell me a story about how each one was purchased over the course of many years. They tell me that their vision is a little blurry with each one. They also say that they get headaches and distorted vision when they change glasses.

These are all the same glasses! The minor differences cause

adjustment problems without any benefit. What should I do in these situations? My fantasy goes as follows: I ask the patient to pick out the pair of glasses he likes the best. After he gives them to me, I put all the other glasses in the bag he brought them in. I put it on the floor and raise my big foot above it. I pause. Then I stomp on that darn bag really hard. I crush all those useless pairs of glasses that are causing so much trouble. I feel liberated from the confusing problem of explaining that they are all essentially the same. I don't have to explain that this poor person has purchased thousands of dollars of useless glasses. I can just say, "Oh, they don't work! Just use the one you like. It doesn't matter. Everything is okay now. *Tudo bom*," I say in Brazilian Portuguese. "Don't worry, be happy. Just use that pair you like." Sadly, I've never yet done this. But someday . . .

The No LASIK Scam

These same people come in explaining that because their eyes have been constantly changing so much, they cannot have LASIK. Of course, you would only want to operate once to solve a problem. They tell me that someday, when their eyes stop changing, they want to have LASIK and get rid of their need for glasses. Then they will not have to buy $500 to $1500 dollars worth of glasses every year. When I tell them they can have LASIK now, they look at me in disbelief. When they ask me why, I answer like this: "Imagine your job was to sell glasses. If people asked you if they should do something that would make them no longer need glasses, what would the answer be? Some people would say, "No, not yet. Keep spending hundreds of dollars every year here." After they understand that they can have LASIK and no longer need glasses, they usually ask why it costs $2,000 per eye! In my fantasy world, I usually say, "Oh, never mind. Just keep spending fifteen hundred dollars every year for the rest of your life. Of course, you will still be blind without glasses, but at least no one will take advantage of you financially."

Recommendations

So after learning all this about glasses, what should you actually do? Well, it depends on what you want. If you are an older guy like me and you just want a pair that will last, get metal frames and glass lenses. In this same situation, get standard single focus bifocals. Set the focus around 18 inches from your face.

Why would I suggest this approach for these people? First

of all, metal frames last a long time. Sometimes people come in with steel frames that they have been using for eight to ten years! "Isn't glass heavier than plastic?" you might ask. Yes, it is. So if you have very thick lenses, it should be avoided because they will fall down your nose even more than they would if you got plastic. But if they are not very thick and you want them to last, get glass. It doesn't scratch as much.

What about coatings for these lenses? We know that ultraviolet light is bad. But a second pair of the same type of lenses as sunglasses would solve that problem. The trouble with all coatings is that they eventually wear off. When they do, it creates a very irregular lens surface. This eventually reduces the quality of vision. Then you have to buy a new pair.

"But what if I just want the best glasses ever, and someone else is paying?" In that case, I would start with the frames. They should be comfortable and fit well. They should be appropriately stylish. The frame should be made of a material that is strong, yet adjustable. This material should be able to keep its shape so that it will continue to be well adjusted to your face. It should be durable enough that when you drop them, they won't break or fall out of adjustment.

As far as lenses go, high-index plastic lenses are the thinnest and therefore the lightest. They take coatings well. Which coatings should you get? Get ultraviolet for sure. UV rays cause skin cancer and wrinkles. They are probably involved in macular degeneration and cataracts. So you want to reduce them as much as possible. Interestingly, this coating doesn't change the color of the lens. It is clear. There is no noticeable change in the colors you see. Also, glasses lenses cause reflections. In my own experience, antiglare and antireflective coatings both improve visual quality. What about scratch-resistant coating? Fine, go ahead. But remember that they still can scratch, and they eventually will.

What about children? Well, they should have polycarbonate lenses. These are a type of safety glass. Just by the nature of being a child, accidents are likely. Since we want to protect their eyes, we always recommend this lens material.

All right, so you are buying this great pair of glasses. How do you make sure you don't have all the problems I've been discussing? This is best answered with a list.

1. Don't change the axis of astigmatism.
2. Make sure each lens is not over-minused.
3. Have the optical center of each lens marked with ink.

Look at yourself in the mirror while wearing the new glasses. Make sure the ink dots line up with the middle of your eyes.

4. Make sure the bifocal starts in the right place for you. This is most likely at the same place on your body as the last glasses. This is not the same place on the glasses. You have to put the glasses on and look in the mirror. Or, if it is your first pair of bifocals, try to start the bifocal lens at the edge of your lower eyelid.

5. Make sure you see significantly better with this new lens power in each eye.

6. When you first get them, have them checked to make sure they are the power that was prescribed.

7. If you are changing lens power, get one pair at a time. Make sure you like them before buying more.

Story

By Rick Miller

When I first saw Dr. May about ten years ago, I had two cataracts removed, followed by some LASIK work. Over the years, my eyes would require stronger lenses, which is perfectly normal.

About six or eight months ago, I found my right eye getting tired after a short amount of reading or a half hour looking at the computer screen. The other doctor in the office worked with me, trying to get my eyes to function after changing several pairs of glasses. After trying different prescriptions, I then gave up. I simply closed my right eye, the one that seemed to get tired quickly, and just used my left eye. I was able to read longer just using one eye, either the left or the right. By then, I realized that I could use my right eye to read as well with my left eye closed. With both eyes open, I was seeing two different images. I brought that to Dr. May's attention. He did a lot of tests and finally put some lens in front of my eyes, and I was no longer seeing double vision. He explained something about prisms and moving the two images together so my brain saw only one. When I got the first pair of glasses with the prism built on it, I was able to read almost immediately. It took me a few moments to get the right distance from what I was reading, but soon I was able to read very small letters with both eyes open.

I often sit in front of the monitor for hours without my eyes feeling tired. Good man, Dr. May.

Comments

Rick Miller had a tendency for double vision unrelated to glasses. It's not that rare. As many as 85% of the people out there have a tendency to develop this problem. If the glasses are not made perfectly with the center of the lens over the middle of the eye, double vision can occur in these people.

When Rick first arrived to see me, he had a combination of this tendency for his eyes to cross, along with the wrong glasses. By centering his lenses and adding some prisms, we moved the images together so he sees one.

He had a careful examination and proper analysis after prior unsuccessful attempts in other locations. Eye doctors don't make a profit by remaking glasses. Spending time with someone to find out what is wrong is a money loser, a commercial thing. Some eye doctors want to make glasses and make money. A more personal approach will result in a better diagnosis but less money for the doctor.

Chapter 8

Refractive Surgery

Refractive surgery is a confusing alphabet soup of abbreviations. To add to the problem, once you find out what these letters stand for, the words still don't make sense! Who uses keratomileusis (the "K" in LASIK and LASEK) in a sentence?

To understand how all these things work, we have to talk a little bit about the structure of the front of the eye. We know that the eye is like a camera. The front is like a lens, but it is actually a two-lens system. The clear part in the front of the eye, the cornea, provides two-thirds of its focusing power. Then there is the colored part of the eye called the iris. The circular opening in the middle of the iris is called the pupil. This opens and closes to adjust the amount of light entering the eye.

Immediately behind the pupil is the lens. It provides the other third of the focusing power.

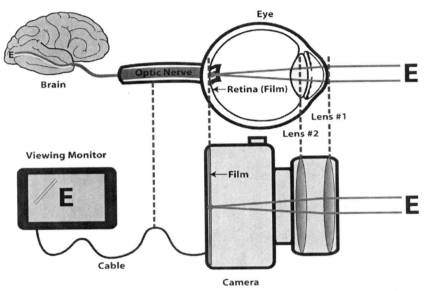

Camera - Brain Analogy

The eye is like a video camera with a view screen. The front is like the adjustable lens system of a video camera on autofocus. When something comes close, the camera automatically adjusts its focus to see near. Then the film on the video camera creates an image which is then sent back to the brain through a cable. The transmission through this cable carries the image all the way to the video monitor at the back of the brain.

The cornea has a surface that is like skin. This is called the epithelium. It can grow back really fast if removed. Below this is a part that is like bone. This structural part of the cornea is called the stroma. When you remove this, it doesn't grow back.

Instead, it usually (but not always) forms a cloudy scar. Refractive surgery involves reshaping this bone-like tissue so that it focuses differently.

How we reshape the cornea has changed dramatically over the last twenty years.

RK (Radial Keratotomy)

The story of refractive surgery starts with the Soviet Union. In that era, the communist government of Russia didn't want to pay for glasses for its people. The solution was radial keratotomy (RK). By giving this surgery to everyone with myopia (nearsightedness), they didn't have to pay for glasses. The trouble was that surgery caused a lot of problems. But the existence of these problems was treated as a state secret. All we heard in the U.S. was how the superior Soviet medical system cured the need for glasses without any complications! This was a surprise for American medicine, because never before in history had there ever been a surgery without any potential problems.

I remember watching the *60 Minutes* news show during the '80s when they were interviewing the developer of radial keratotomy. I was shocked that Mike Wallace was just nodding in agreement when Dr. Fyodorov claimed to have a surgery that worked every time without complications. I remember turning to my wife, also a medical student at the time, and saying that if he were an American doctor, Mike Wallace would tear him apart for that statement.

Radial keratotomy generated a lot of interest in the U.S. medical community in the 1980s. Two schools of thought appeared. One was that we don't know enough about this procedure. We should study it more before we start to perform it on a large scale. The other was that it works great! So pay me $3,000 to perform this surgery on as many people as I can.

A really great study called the Prospective Evaluation of Radial Keratotomy was coordinated at USC by the famous Dr. Peter McDonnell and others in the early 1990s. This study showed that there actually were a lot of potential problems with this surgery. It also showed that if done a certain way in carefully chosen individuals, it did work fairly well.

Just after Dr. McDonnell figured out how we should do this surgery, suddenly a new technology arrived. Dr. Stephen Trokel in New York discovered that an ultraviolet laser normally used to cut plastic could reshape the surface of the eye without causing damage. There was so little damage that the cornea remained completely clear after being reshaped by this laser.

This was revolutionary, because every time we made a cut on the cornea before this point, a cloudy scar formed. These cloudy scars in the clear part of the front of the eye can cause glare, astigmatism, double vision, and blindness. For the first time, this laser allowed us to reshape the eye's surface without losing its clarity. Now we could adjust the focusing power of the eye by essentially grinding a contact lens onto its surface. This procedure was called photorefractive keratectomy (PRK). Again, in cooperation with others, Dr. McDonnell (while still at USC) made great contributions to mankind by proving that this worked and showing all of us how to do the treatment. This treatment started a revolution. It exploded onto the international stage. Suddenly these lasers were popping up in every country.

PRK (Photorefractive Keratectomy)

PRK is a treatment on the outer surface of the eye. It hurts a lot and takes about two weeks to work. The pain is caused by removing a large circular area of the surface of the cornea. The removal of the epithelium, or skin-like outer surface, is what causes the pain. After this is removed, the bone-like structural part (the stroma) is reshaped. Then the epithelium rapidly covers the surface while the underlying stroma remains clear and permanently reshaped. Once we are done with the treatment, people have what is basically a large scrape on the front of the eye. This hurts. I know; I had it done. Then we have to wait for the surface to heal. The pain usually gets a lot better after one day. During this day, the surface of the eye heals to a point where the scrape is much smaller, so it hurts less. In the next day or two, the eye is usually completely covered with one layer of cells, so the pain stops because the scrape is gone. The vision usually takes two weeks to come back. It takes this long for the surface to smooth out and swelling to go away.

Besides pain, another problem associated with PRK is something called haze. This is a scarring that sometimes develops on the cornea after PRK. It usually happens when treating someone with really thick glasses or if there is suddenly much more ultraviolet light on the eyes. This would happen when people who had PRK in the cold, cloudy northeastern United States went on a vacation in some sunny place. They would sometimes come home with hazy vision from this clouding on the outermost part of the eye. Happily, this clouding usually goes away with time. However, sometimes it doesn't. Because haze is more common if someone has very thick glasses, in these people we often recommend LASIK.

LASIK (Laser in situ Keratomileusis)

Although we finally had something that could reliably improve vision without glasses, it still hurt a lot and took a long time to work. This procedure was essentially replaced by LASIK because it hurts much less and works a lot faster. LASIK involves making a very thin protective flap of the cornea, lifting it up and applying the laser to the underlying cornea. We use the same ultraviolet (excimer) laser, but the reshaping happens 30% deeper. That is, partway down from the very surface of the cornea. Once the surface is reshaped, the flap is replaced. The whole cornea then takes on a new shape. That way, the cornea is reshaped without leaving the surface bare. This causes much less pain and much quicker visual recovery. Sadly, this surgery was further developed and popularized in the United States at our cross-town rival UCLA by Dr. Robert Maloney.

Microkeratome and Creation of a Flap

The advantage and disadvantage of LASIK is the creation of

a protective flap. The surgical creation of this flap can cause problems. The machine that creates this flap is called a microkeratome. This machine attaches to the eye through suction. Then a vibrating blade automatically creates the flap. This usually takes about a minute.

This flap may also be created by a laser. This is called Intralase®. The result of both of these techniques is to create a trapdoor-like shape. When the trap door is raised, 70% of the thickness of the cornea is still below. This flap, or trapdoor, is made up of corneal epithelium and stroma. When this trapdoor is raised, it remains attached to the cornea at a hinge. After the cornea under the flap is reshaped by the laser, we lay this flap back down to cover the treated structural part of the eye. The flap then takes on the new shape. Amazingly, it sticks quite well. At first, the attachment is not very strong. Rubbing the eye during the first three days can cause a lot of problems. The surface of the eye can easily be moved out of position and wrinkled. Then the vision gets really bad. If this happens, we have to replace the flap. We usually smooth out the wrinkles by purposefully causing lots of swelling of the flap. Think of this like blowing up an air mattress. Then we lay this inflated, non-wrinkled flap back down in position. If a person doesn't rub it, vision usually comes back quite well. Unfortunately, sometimes, no matter how well we take care of people with wrinkled flaps, the wrinkles stay and distort vision. So if you have LASIK done, don't rub your eyes, and wear a shield at night.

Infection is always possible when an incision is made. This is true of both incisions made with blades and lasers. Infections in the cornea are more serious when they are closer to the inside of the eye. Once an infection penetrates into the middle of the eye, the chance of blindness is much greater. Because infections are deeper into the eye when they occur below a LASIK flap, they are more serious. This may lead to permanent visual loss.

These two problems bring up the issue of bilateral treatments. If a patient gets an infection, his vision can go way down. After the treatment on both eyes, if a person has one of these complications on both sides, it will result in poor vision in both eyes! This is much worse than when vision is down in one eye. These people have trouble working. They go from functional to nonfunctional.

DLK (Diffuse Lamellar Keratitis)

DLK is an inflammation without infection in the area

between the inner part of the flap and the resurfaced cornea below. It causes blurred vision because of swelling and irritation in this area. It is usually treated well with eye drop medications. If this happens, clear vision can be delayed for quite some time. These eyes may have more leftover nearsightedness (myopia).

LASIK caused an explosion in the number of treatments. Suddenly we had a relatively safe, comfortable, and effective way to improve vision without glasses. The result is usually stable for a very long time. What used to be revolutionary has now become routine. And it continues to get better.

Wavefront Analysis and Customized Ablation

When the excimer laser first came out, we used the glasses prescription to program this computer-driven laser. This is information we get by asking which lens seems clearer. We used a person's judgment about fine details of vision with different lenses. The trouble is, sometimes it's hard to know which lenses make you see better. There is some guessing involved by both the doctor and patient in this process. Now we still do this to double-check the treatment plan provided by a wavefront analyzer.

Wavefront technology involves the use of reflected light from inside the eye to determine how the eye focuses. With this type of measurement, we can develop an individualized treatment. The exact shape of an eye is like a fingerprint. Everyone is a little different. If its shape is slightly irregular, focusing can be irregular. Also, inside the eye is the natural lens. This internal lens may itself be irregular. By using reflections of light coming back out of the eye, we can treat a person according to how the whole eye focuses. These reflections tell us how the lens and the cornea work together. This information is collected by something called a wavefront analyzer. Then this information is converted into a customized treatment plan to compensate for irregularities of the whole focusing system. The excimer laser then applies laser light in this specific individualized pattern. Like everything these days, this is all computerized. The collection of this information, its processing to generate a laser treatment plan, and the applications of this laser are all done by computer.

LASEK (Laser Subepithelial Keratomileusis)

This is yet another way to use the excimer laser. In this

procedure, we go back to reshaping the outermost part of the eye. The location for this treatment is the same as in PRK. The difference is that a machine is used to raise a flap of only the skin-like surface of the eye (corneal epithelium). After the structural part of the eye is reshaped, the epithelium is laid back down to cover the surface. The idea here is to avoid making a flap of the structural part of the cornea while not causing the pain of PRK. Some studies do show decreased pain, while others don't. Also, visual recovery is slower. This technology has not gained a lot of popularity, and this is probably because LASIK works so well.

CK (Conductive Keratoplasty)

The problem with LASIK is that we have to use an excimer laser. These lasers are extremely expensive. Even if you own one, you still may have to pay a software fee of hundreds of dollars each time you use it. This expense influenced the development of focusing treatments that don't require an expensive laser.

CK involves placing heat energy to the cornea by hand. This causes the cornea to contract where the heat is applied. If a circle of treatments is applied on the cornea, the center can bulge forward. This makes the eye more nearsighted, allowing it to see near more easily. CK can be used to treat small amounts of farsightedness or to cause nearsightedness to help older people read without glasses.

AK (Astigmatic Keratotomy)

This is a method of treating astigmatism. Remember, astigmatism occurs when there is a shallow curvature on one part of the dome of the cornea. There is a steeper curve ninety degrees away. This is like a football cut in half lengthwise. If incisions are made paralleling the outer border of the cornea off to the side, the steeper curve can be flattened. That way, the curvature can be the same all the way around the cornea. Its shape becomes more like a basketball cut in half, creating better focus.

These incisions are commonly used around the time of cataract surgery. Cataract surgery involves putting a new lens inside the eye. Nearsightedness or farsightedness can be corrected by using just the right power artificial lens. These lenses usually don't correct for astigmatism. By adding this treatment to cataract surgery, we can make people see better without glasses.

CLE (Clear Lens Extraction)

Some people are not very good refractive surgery candidates. When someone is very nearsighted or very farsighted, refractive surgery can cause lots of glare problems. There is a limit to the amount of treatment each individual can have. If someone needs a very large amount of treatment, he may be better off having his lens removed and replaced with an artificial lens. This is a routine surgery. When someone has cloudiness in his natural lens, it is called a cataract. So, clear lens extraction is doing a cataract surgery when there is no cataract. The focusing power of the eye is improved by changing the lens power inside the eye. With an artificial intraocular lens, these implantable lenses are individualized to correct the focusing power of the eye.

The trouble with doing this type of surgery is that the flexibility of the natural lens is lost. Remember, this flexibility is what allows the eye to change its focus to see near. If someone is older than 45 and needs bifocals to read anyway, he is not losing much in terms of focusing ability.

It is possible to implant a bifocal lens at this point. Then one would be able to see near and far. These lenses are hard to put into someone who has not had cataracts because they cause some decreased visual quality.

Then the next issue is that clear lens extraction is an operation inside the eye. This type of surgery takes risks that just don't exist with other refractive procedures. Infection inside the eye is possible here. If this happens, permanent untreatable blindness often occurs. Cataract surgery on people with lots of nearsightedness carries a higher risk of retinal detachment. This is also a potentially blinding problem and requires surgery to fix. Sometimes nothing works to fix a retinal detachment.

Intraocular Contact Lens

If someone has a cataract and wears very thick glasses, surgery to fix the cataract is often a great solution. The risks are then justified, because if we do not operate, the patient eventually goes blind anyway. After cataract surgery, the new artificial lens often dramatically improves vision without glasses.

The Bait-and-Switch LASIK Scam

When you see LASIK offered for prices that seem too good

to be true, watch out. It might be a bait-and-switch scam. The bait is the low price. Once you bite by going to the office, the switch begins. Each part of the process of doing a medical procedure is divided up. Prices are assigned to what is usually included in a standard procedure. For example, you might want someone to examine you before the surgery to decide exactly what to do and to make sure the surgery will not harm you. If so, you pay extra. If you want to be examined after the surgery to make sure you are not developing any complications, that will be extra. If you have astigmatism or higher degrees of myopia or farsightedness, that costs more. If you need re-treatment, you start over at the beginning of the costs. Because it is cheaper to have someone other than the surgeon examine you before and after the surgery, you probably will not meet the operating doctor. Of course, he or she will be there to perform the procedure. All your questions will be answered by "counselors" who have no medical training.

These businesses are only open during the day, so emergency problems like pain or flap dislocations have to be worked on during business hours. If this happens, of course that costs more.

When I first heard of this approach, I was amazed. The

professional approach to any medical procedure is to do the best job you can. That includes careful evaluation before any surgery to make sure it is a good idea. A careful plan is made by the operating doctor. The operating surgeon examines the patient. He or she talks with the patient to make sure he understands the risks. Then the same surgeon performs the procedure. After the surgery, the same doctor evaluates the patient to make sure things are going well. They may prescribe additional treatments to fine-tune the vision. They look for potential problems at the times when they might occur. Usually, additional treatments are done without additional doctor charges. Sometimes there may be a facility fee.

This is quite a lot of work. That is why it usually costs at least $2,000, including the facility fee. At the center I use, the facility fee is around $800. The doctor makes the rest. That's not much to restore someone's vision permanently. Glasses often cost $500, and you have to keep getting glasses and contact lenses your whole life. Without them, you cannot see.

The "Co-management" Scam

An active LASIK surgeon is the best person to check you to

make a surgical plan. No one else is experienced enough to know if you are a good candidate. The experience of checking people before surgery, doing the surgery, and then taking care of them after surgery cannot be matched for the best results. Any deviation from this approach is a reduction in quality.

If you want to make money with LASIK but are not allowed to do so by law, don't know how, or don't want to bother, you can "co-manage." That means you send the patient to someone else to do the surgery. You check them before and after. This justifies your making money from the procedure. It is not really a "kickback." Nooooo.

My Own Refractive Surgery Story

I started playing baseball when I was five. Some of my most vivid childhood memories are of hot, dusty days playing baseball in the deep south of the United States. I remember the hot summer days, the brown-red dirt of Mississippi, and the bright sunlight reflecting from my clean white uniform. The thrill of ice water, soft drinks, and popsicles after the game is still vivid.

As I got older, the skills of the other players improved, while mine seemed to stagnate. My coaches decided that catching fly balls was something I just couldn't do. No matter how much practice they gave me, I just couldn't learn. They noticed, however, that I could catch balls thrown directly to me quite well. Also, I seemed to be able to handle ground balls in my direction. They decided to play me at first base. The coaches would often remind me that even though I was right-handed, they were putting me at a position reserved for left-handers because I couldn't play anywhere else.

Because I was nearsighted, I could see the general course of the ball. I could move to where it should be and wait for the ball to come into focus. Then, once I could see the ball, I was able react quickly to what I could see and make the catch.

As I search my memory now, I remember having my right foot on first base and looking at the short stop fielding the ball with anxiety. I remember concentrating on watching him in a blur. Then that hazy image would throw the ball toward me. After a delay, the ball would suddenly come into focus around the pitcher's mound. Then I would react quickly to make the catch. Each time an infielder would make a throw to first, I would wait for the ball to come into focus, make a quick adjustment, and then make the catch. At that time, I thought this was the way everyone else was seeing the ball.

My hitting was average at best. I struck out a lot. When I did get hits, they were usually ground balls to first base or fly balls over the first baseman's head. But my "at bats" tended to be very long. I would foul the ball to the first base side two or three times. The pitcher had to make lots of pitches to get me out. Finally I would hit a fair ball toward the first baseman or strike out.

Sometimes the coaches would keep me on the bench. They would put me in late in the game because they had to play everyone. I have a vivid memory of a night game playing in left field when a hit was made. I knew it was a hit by the crack of the bat and the roar of the crowd. Everyone looked my way, so I knew it was my responsibility to catch the ball. Searching the sky, I suddenly saw the ball rocketing down twenty feet away. My sprinting diving lunge was in vain. I missed! The crowd moaned, and the children ran frantically around the bases as I chased the ball and made a long throw toward the infield.

It was around this time, at the age of nine, when I was riding in a car with my mother and asked her if she could see a sign in the distance. When she said, "Yes, of course," I asked her if something was wrong with my eyes. I couldn't see that road sign! She took me to an eye doctor, and I got glasses. When I put them on, I was amazed that I could see the individual leaves on trees. Everything seemed so available, so immediate. It was all suddenly there in front of me. The clarity was overwhelming.

Suddenly, my baseball performance improved! I could watch the ball from the hit to the shortstop. I could see him catch the ball. I could see him start to throw. I could see the ball coming out of his hand. I could track the ball from his hand. I didn't have to make a last-minute adjustment. It was suddenly easy to catch the throws to first base! Balls hit at me were also easy. I had so much time to react! It was almost like the game was in slow motion.

Suddenly, I was the best hitter on the team. I went from a substitute player to batting fourth. I could see the ball leave the pitcher's hand. My reaction was so quick that I could make a full swing. I discovered that I could hit the ball hard. I could even wait for pitches and plan where I would place the hits! I went from a marginal player to the best on the team, in one year. It was the miracle of clear vision that propelled me to an all-star little league baseball player.

The trouble was that I had to wear glasses. That was okay in baseball, but other sports were difficult. Specifically, at that age

I made a transition to football. I dressed in pads and a helmet while I played football as a ten-year-old. I tried to wear glasses, but they didn't fit inside the helmet. So once again, I was back to not seeing during sports.

Luckily, there was a position in football perfect for someone who was nearsighted. That was the line. In that type of position, you play three feet away from your opponent. You know where he is at all times. In that position, the game occurs in a very small space. You don't need to see far away to wrestle with someone directly in front of you. Many efforts to move to the tight end where I could catch passes failed because I couldn't see the ball coming out of the quarterback's hand. When I tried to wear contact lenses, the front of the helmet would come down on my eyes and knock the contact lenses off. After embarrassing searches for my clear contact lenses by the whole team in the dirt of the practice field at dusk, I gave up on wearing contact lenses in football.

Much later, after becoming a doctor, I had the great honor of being allowed into one of the greatest ophthalmology training programs in the world. There were only four of us entering this rarified position out of about 200 applicants at USC. When we arrived, it was fascinating to notice that the four of us were all quite nearsighted. In fact, I was the least nearsighted of the four. It seemed to me that we were motivated to solve the problem of poor vision. We could understand visual loss like no one else. We knew how restricting it was in our own lives. I think we each chose this field to address the problems we had suffered as children.

After my training at USC, in the early part of my actual practice of ophthalmology, I had the honor of being trained to perform refractive procedures by the great Peter McDonnell, M.D. He developed the beginnings of what the public now thinks of as LASIK. (He may be the greatest ophthalmologist in the world, after maybe a few others.) Suddenly, thanks to Dr. McDonnell and a few other doctors, the world had a good procedure to cure nearsightedness. I remember looking through the microscope as I was performing this procedure with the excimer laser and thinking that this was a miracle! I wanted it for myself.

After Dr. McDonnell did this procedure to cure my myopia, my life changed. By then, my sports were tennis, skiing, surfing, snorkeling, and boating. Suddenly, everything was better. I didn't need contact lenses! I could surf and swim without worrying that my contact lenses would wash out of my eyes in the ocean. When the high winds blew in my face while boating on the ocean, I didn't have to worry that my lenses would blow out. While skiing, the dry cold winds would not blow the contact lenses out of my eyes. I no longer had the nagging worry that I would be lost in the snow without vision to find my way out.

Immediately after my vision correction surgery, however, I noticed that I had "night glare." I had only one eye done at a time. That way, if something went wrong with the first, I didn't have to have the second done. I could still rely on my good, non-operated eye if there was a problem. It was really interesting to have night glare in one eye and a non-operated eye on the other side. Of course, I had a contact lens on my un-operated eye. At night I noticed that yes, I had a strange glare effect on my operated eye. There was a strange flare around lights. Please remember that I was doing this surgery when I had it performed on myself.

It was my responsibility to explain the potential problems to my patients. Night glare was something I had explained to my patients as a potential complication many times. I had never experienced this problem. Now I had glare! The bizarre thing was that my vision was actually much more clear and vivid in the operated eye with night glare! The other eye had a contact lens and 20/20 vision. The lasered eye with night glare seemed better.

Here is a secret of laser vision correction. Vision is much clearer without a contact lens! If you see 20/20 with a contact lens, that is not as good as 20/20 vision without a contact lens. If you go onto the Internet, you can find lots of complaints about night glare after LASIK. The hidden secret you will not find on the Internet is that vision with night glare without a contact lens is much better than vision without night glare with a contact lens. The reason for this is that if you have good vision naturally, and you put a layer of plastic on your eye, you will not see as well. The plastic of the contact lens causes its own problems with visual quality. Nothing is better than good vision without contact lenses or glasses.

Another thing I discovered after my vision correction surgery was that I had made many adjustments throughout my life, thinking that it wasn't that bad to be nearsighted. Suddenly, after I was no longer nearsighted, I saw what a profound effect it had had on my life. I was suddenly free! I could wake up and see! I could surf, play tennis, and drive a car with much better vision than before. A problem that had taken a lifetime of adjustment was gone!

LASIK is liberating and life-changing. Clear vision is something we all experience on a moment-to-moment basis. It is one of the most wonderful things in life! Getting refractive surgery was one of the best decisions of my life. I remember thinking that this was much more valuable than a car! The price of $4,000 was a bargain. Thank you once again, Dr. McDonnell.

Recommendations

- If you don't mind pain, and if you only have a little correction in your glasses, consider surface treatment with the excimer laser. If you have more than four units of nearsightedness or two units of farsightedness, have LASIK. Laser treatments with the excimer laser are more stable and predictable. Don't bother with anything else unless you have a very large amount of myopia.

- If you have very thick lenses, consult your ophthalmologist to find out if the treatment would work.

- Avoid high-volume discount LASIK centers like the plague.

- Make sure the doctor who will do the surgery checks you before and after the treatment.

Comments

By Laura McDonnell, one of the editors

Remember, nothing is free! LASIK procedures require incredibly delicate machinery that is hard to build and has to be constantly kept in top condition to ensure everything goes right. Whether the doctor rents or buys, the money they need to do so has to come from somewhere, and that's on top of the software fee!

For the doctors to stay in business doing LASIK, they need to at least break even, like in any other business. Another expense is that doctors, like machines, are expensive to make and need to stay in top condition. If you remember having to pay back student loans to go to college, doctors require many more years of training, and even when they graduate, they still have to take additional courses of whatever type so that they stay aware of new methods, like the LASIK procedure, that their patients need to know. If they don't take enough classes, they can have their right to practice medicine taken away because it's a sign that they aren't able to give their patients the care they need.

LASIK surgeons, as specialists, have to have even more

training than the general doctor. That is why you need to make sure to be examined by one.

And then there's office space, advertising, and the more normal business expenses. As you can see, doing a LASIK procedure takes a lot of money. That money has to come from somewhere. So if you hear a price that's too good to be true, it probably is.

Chapter 9

Diabetes and the Eye

Blindness used to be common in diabetes. Because it runs in families, many of my diabetic patients have an aunt or uncle who went blind. Usually these were people who did not see an ophthalmologist until it was too late. They had something called diabetic retinopathy. This means a problem in the retina caused by diabetes. Using our camera analogy, the retina is like film in the camera of the eye. If a camera has no film, or if the film is defective, the picture cannot be formed. Then you can't see.

The retina is an amazing thing. This part of the body takes the light coming into the eye and changes it into information the brain can understand. The retina is so important that some doctors dedicate their whole careers to this one very small, important part of the eye (like my good friend Glen Jarus, M.D.). The retina is the part that creates vision. It is made of permanent cells that cannot be replaced. Diabetes threatens this critical body part. A large amount of our effort to keep diabetic people seeing involves watching over and caring for the retina.

What is diabetes?

After absorbing food, the body converts it to sugar. It sends this energy source to all the cells in the body through the bloodstream. Sugar is the food the cells eat.

Diabetes is a disease caused by not having enough of a certain hormone called insulin. This hormone allows sugar to get from the blood into all the cells. It acts like a key to unlock the door for food delivery. It is an essential key, because without it, the cells starve and die. Again, these permanent cells cannot be replaced.

In diabetes, the sugar (called glucose) builds up inside the blood because of the lack of the hormone called insulin to allow sugar into the cells. Sugar continues to be made and sent out into the blood. It just can't arrive, because there is no key to unlock the door to let it in. That key is insulin. The lack of this hormone is what causes diabetes. Sugar is sent out into the blood, but it can't be delivered, so it builds up.

The whole body is made of cells. That includes the blood vessels. Cells are the basic building blocks of the whole body. A traffic jam of sugar in the bloodstream causes damage to the blood vessels. When this happens in the eye, the blood vessels that feed the retina get damaged. The cells that make up the blood vessels also get damaged because they can't get any food. So both the high levels of sugar and the lack of food damage the cells of the blood vessels. These damaged blood vessels leak and die.

The blood vessels also carry oxygen for the cells to breathe. So if the blood vessels die from diabetes, the retina cannot eat or breathe. This causes parts of the retina to die. Because they are permanent cells, they can never be replaced.

Diabetic Retinopathy

Nonproliferative Diabetic Retinopathy

Nonproliferative diabetic retinopathy is a condition where the small blood vessels of the retina are leaking and disappearing. Fluid from the blood vessels is leaking out into the retina. The retina is such a finely designed structure that any change in its shape causes it not to work as well as it could.

Also, if cholesterol from the blood leaks out and collects in the center of the retina, it will permanently damage the structure of the central retina. This area, the macula, is where all detail vision starts. A permanent change in its structure causes permanent bad vision.

Diabetes damages the lining of these blood vessels. When this happens, they leak and disappear. Remember, these are pipes that stuff is flowing through. If they leak, the pipes' contents spill out into the retina. Some of these contents do not belong in the retina. Everything has to be in just the right place for the retina to work well. When fluid leaks out of the blood vessels into the retina, the structure is changed. This happens as a result of swelling with fluid from the bloodstream or the permanent deposit of cholesterol into the retina. Loss of these small blood vessels also causes retinal nerve cells to die. We can't put back lost blood vessels and nerve cells; we can only try to slow or stop their loss.

The result of this change in structure is that the function of the retina is disrupted. Some of this bad stuff (cholesterol) builds up and cannot be removed by the body. If this happens, the structure of the retina is permanently disrupted, and you will never see well again. Loss of blood vessels and nerve cells can only be treated by keeping blood sugar, blood pressure, and cholesterol controlled and avoiding smoking.

The reason you have to come in before your vision goes bad is that we can see these blood vessels leaking before you notice that your vision is blurry. That is when you want us to identify the leaks that are going to cause decreased vision. We can plug theses leaks with a laser. If everything works out all right, you never have to suffer poor vision. We are not very good at recovering vision that is lost from diabetes. We are pretty good at preventing loss of vision if we treat when vision is threatened but not yet lost.

Treatment for Nonproliferative Diabetic Retinopathy

In general, treatments for diabetes tend to stabilize vision. It is less common to improve vision. That is why you want to see an ophthalmologist before you have problems. Then we can stabilize your vision at a good level. Treatment is a combination of efforts by the patient, diabetic doctor, and ophthalmologist. It has been proven that very good control of blood sugar, blood pressure, and cholesterol (weight loss can help all of these) and avoidance of smoking will slow, but not reverse, the development of diabetic retinopathy.

Proliferative Diabetic Retinopathy

If this problem is not treated with a laser, it almost always causes blindness in an eye. In diabetes, blood vessels that supply oxygen to the retina disappear. Then the retina can't breathe. Parts of the retina that can't breathe send a message to the body to grow new blood vessels. If this happens in your arm, these new vessels are nice! They provide new oxygen and food for the cells. But in the eye, everything has to be in just the right place to work. When these new blood vessels are formed, they grow across the retina. They are more than just new vessels. These new blood vessels require support, and this support is a type of scar. The new vessels grow as part of an expanding scar. This scar is attached to the retina and to the vitreous gel that fills the hollow center of the eye.

Scars do interesting things. First they grow. Then they contract. When the support structure for these new vessels contracts, it causes the new blood vessels to break and bleed. Scar contraction also pulls the retina out of position and away from its outer blood supply. This is another reason it stops working. Proliferative retinopathy occurs due to production of VEGF. This is like a hormone produced by parts of the retina that have lost blood vessels and aren't getting enough oxygen and nutrients.

The peripheral part of the retina doesn't see detail. We use it for side vision. If we sacrifice some of this peripheral retina by treating with laser, we cut down the production of VEGF. Then the bad blood vessels usually stop growing and shrivel up. Laser cuts the risk of severe visual loss from these blood vessels. We do, however, sacrifice some night and peripheral vision by treating the outer retina. This is a small price to pay for preventing blindness. Unfortunately, laser cannot be used to treat loss of blood vessels and nerve cells in the macula. Blurry vision caused by this part of diabetic retinopathy is not treatable.

Sometimes bleeding keeps happening and laser treatment to control the proliferative retinopathy cannot be done, or we get the retinopathy late and we find retinal detachment has occurred. In these severe cases, surgery called vitrectomy is sometimes used to remove the bloody gel from the eye, take away the scar tissue, treat the retina with laser, and reattach it by pushing it back in place with a gas bubble. This surgery can save many eyes but has greater risk and side effects than if we can treat with laser earlier in the course of this disease.

Cataracts and Diabetes

Another problem that may be caused by diabetes is cataracts. Because concentrations of sugar build up in diabetes, it can get into places where it isn't needed. When it gets into the lens, sugar causes the lens to swell. Swelling changes how the lens focuses. If a diabetic with uncontrolled sugar needs glasses, the glasses stop working because the eye focuses differently with a swollen lens. This is why people with diabetes say that their vision goes bad when their sugar has been out of control. Once they get their blood glucose back to a normal level, the sugar gradually leaves the lens. Then the swelling goes away, and the lens focuses the way it usually does. Their glasses work again.

This can take weeks if the sugar is completely controlled. Usually, it is not. That delays the return of the lens to where it used to be. These people come in asking for new glasses. Being a friendly, agreeable guy, I like to give my patients what they want. The trouble is, glasses don't change. They are made of glass or plastic. Once we make them, they always focus the same way. If I give someone with uncontrolled blood sugar new glasses, the glasses will eventually be the wrong power because the eye will change back to how it used to be. Then people see like they used to with their old glasses. The new glasses don't work.

I hear this story often from people who have left their other eye doctors and are coming to me for the first time. They say that their old glasses work better than the new $500 pair they got in their previous eye doctor's office. When I ask if their sugar was high around the time they got their new glasses, they usually say, "Yes, it was, but now it's okay." Then they ask, "If my sugar is now at a good level, shouldn't my glasses work?"

When diabetics continue to have sugar levels that are out of control, the lens swells and shrinks over and over again, causing damage to the lens. The lens is made of proteins, and these proteins start out clear. They turn cloudy with continued damage from repeated swelling. The lens focuses light. If it becomes cloudy, light can't pass through to be focused. This causes a type of visual loss that can't be helped with glasses. Then, to see again, people need cataract surgery. See the cataract chapter for more information.

Glaucoma and Diabetes

If new blood vessels form in the retina, they may also grow in the front part of the eye. Even after laser or injections of anti-

VEGF drugs, the drainage system can be permanently damaged. If fluid can't get out of the eye, pressure builds up inside the eye. This high pressure can damage the nerve that carries vision. If enough damage occurs, vision will be permanently lost. This is glaucoma.

The type of glaucoma that develops after the growth of these new vessels is one of the worst. It can be impossible to control with the usual treatments. These people often need our most potent types of surgery to control pressure in their eyes.

Recommendations for Diabetic People

Visit your ophthalmologist at least once a year, even if there is nothing wrong that you can detect. After all, before you start losing vision is the best time to nip problems in the bud. If your doctor recommends treatment or testing, get it right away. Keep your blood sugar, blood pressure, and cholesterol as well controlled as you possibly can. When it comes to diabetic retinopathy, smoking is like pouring gasoline on a fire. Do whatever you can to quit the habit.

Chapter 10

The Big three

Dry Eyes, Blepharitis, and Allergies

Okay, so I know I just covered these issues. However, some days it seems that I spend all day discussing these three problems together. People come in because they have eye irritation, fluctuating vision, burning eyes, severe itching, and red-rimmed, swollen eyelids. They have had this problem off and on for many years. They have often seen many doctors about this problem. The antibiotic drops and glasses they received don't seem to help.

When I tell these people they have a mixture of three problems, none of which is curable, they get a panicked look in their eyes. Then I reassure them that none of these problems is serious. By that, I mean that none of them will cause blindness.

None of these problems necessarily means anything bad about their general health. Then we start a long discussion about each one and how they interrelate. That is the subject of this chapter.

Everyone has blepharitis. That is a rather profound statement. Imagine a disease that everyone has. When I realized during my eye training that everyone had this disease, I was amazed. In medical school I had never heard of this disease! Medical training in the United States is standardized. There are things all doctors are supposed to know. We are tested on many different subjects many times before we are allowed to practice medicine. An eye disease everyone has was not part of this when I passed through these tests.

Blepharitis means irritation of the eyelids. Everyone has bacteria growing on their skin. These germs love to grow in places that are warm and wet. That is exactly what it is like on the edge of the eyelid. Bacteria love to grow there. These bacteria fall off the edge of the eyelid onto the surface of the eye. The eye recognizes these germs and responds as if it were infected. That means the eye gets red, tears come out in a flood, and it starts to have a burning sensation. The edge of the eyelids also gets red and itchy.

As if that wasn't bad enough, sometimes the eyelid makes a

toxic chemical that irritates the edge of the eyelid and the eye. Inside the eyelid are factories that make part of the tears (meibomian glands). This stuff is supposed to be toxic to germs invading the eye. It forms the outer of the three layers of tears that protect the eye.

In some people, this outer coating itself is irritating to the eye. If you add this to the bacteria that grow on the edge of the eyelid, it can cause quite a lot of pain. Chronic pain is a very bad thing. It can cause significant personality changes, and in this case, quite a lot of frustration. It keeps coming back!

A specific skin disease causes this problem to be much worse. This is rosacea. This disease seems to be common in people with very light skin. Their skin is very white, and their eyes and the edge of their eyelids are very red. They usually have redness to the cheeks and nose.

This problem can be very difficult to treat. A mixture of pills, medicated eye drops, artificial tears, and special eyelash soaps may be used.

The chronic pain and irritation cause the tear-production system to stop working. Unfortunately, it stops working in a way that causes more eye irritation and pain. Just not having enough tears hurts. When people have a mixture of these three diseases, things that hurt are getting on their eyes. With fewer tears, these particles are not being washed off the eye. So the eye becomes more irritated and hurts more. This leads to a negative cycle where these three issues all make each other worse.

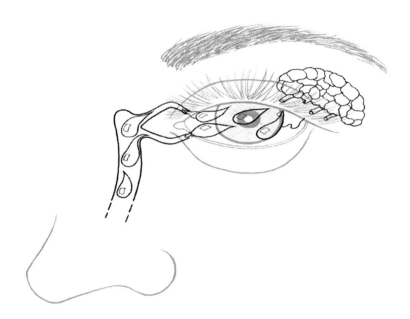

The blink mechanism acts like a pump. It forces fluid out of the lacrimal gland onto the surface of the eye. Also, blinking forces fluid off the eye and into the tear-collecting system. Then the movement of blinking muscles forces fluid out of the tear-collecting system and into the nose.

How This Cycle Develops

1. Germs and toxic chemicals from the eyelid fall onto the eye.

2. The surface of the eye gets irritated.

3. This causes the tear-producing system on the surface of the eye not to work as well.

4. This system makes fewer tears.

5. Airborne pollens land on the eye.

6. The particles don't get washed away quickly because there are fewer tears.

7. Pollens cause an allergic reaction, leading to more irritation.

8. This allergic irritation causes the tear-producing glands to make even fewer tears.

9. Then we start all over again at the top.

Chapter 11

Plastic Surgery

All of us are getting older every day. With age things fall. Tissues stretch out so they can't hold everything up as high or as tightly. On the face there is exposure to ultraviolet light. This causes more breakdown of the skin and its structural support. This process is significant around the eyes for both functional and cosmetic reasons. By functional, we mean how you see. By cosmetic, we mean how you look.

When people are quite young, usually in their twenties, they notice their first wrinkles forming. They usually call them "crow's feet." These are lines that start at the outer corner of the eye and point in all directions. "What are these wrinkles caused by?" you might wonder. Well, wrinkles are lines in the skin above a muscle. They are caused by the contraction of the muscle below that skin. When the muscle contracts, it moves the skin into folds. Because the skin and the muscle are connected, whenever a particular muscle contracts, it moves the skin the same way. After a while, lines develop because the skin keeps getting folded the same way. This is how wrinkles form.

You can get rid of these wrinkles by paralyzing the muscle below. That is what BOTOX® does. It causes the muscle to stop moving. Then the skin stays still. There is no reason for the lines to form, and they quickly go away. The downside to BOTOX® is that it wears off. It usually lasts only three months. The other downside is that it's expensive. This leads to some medical providers overcharging and under-treating.

The BOTOX® Scam
Overcharging, Under-treating, Not Checking Results.

Recently, a patient of mine got a birthday present of a combination of spa treatments. Included with massage, facials, and nails was BOTOX®. When I hear things like this, I wonder how a spa gets a doctor to evaluate a patient, determine a treatment, and prescribe a medication. Of course, the doctor would evaluate the result of that treatment on later visits. That way, the best possible results can be achieved. Then I wonder what kind of doctor would practice in a spa. I guess a plastic surgeon could. But it would have to be a huge place to keep that surgeon busy. I guess a semi-retired doctor who liked to hang out in spas could do it. There just aren't enough of these people to work at all the spas in Southern California. But hey, maybe I could do this when I am semi-retired. This is starting to sound good!

I am sure there are some spas where there is nothing but first-class medical care and excellent spa treatment. If I were having BOTOX®, I would check carefully that I was being correctly evaluated and treated by a qualified physician. The medications should be used as the manufacturer recommends, including expiration dates and storage. There must be a medical chart. You should have a copy of this. That way, other doctors can know what has been done, what has worked, and what has not worked.

Okay, so obviously there aren't a bunch of doctors running around working in spas. That means that the principles of medical practice might be ignored. Could something go wrong? Probably not much. Maybe that's why no one seems to care. But I wouldn't do it for myself. Why not? Well, first I would worry about not getting enough medication to achieve the result. BOTOX® comes in a bottle with a specific amount. It costs around $500 for each bottle wholesale. Each of these bottles has the same tiny bit of dried botulinus toxin (a product of a kind of bacteria). This is the active ingredient in BOTOX®. To give this treatment, sterile salt water is injected into the bottle. Then little bits of the fluid are pulled out of the bottle into syringes. We give these small shots into the areas where the wrinkles are.

So if each bottle costs more than $500, and my patients seem to require at least half a bottle to get the full effect, how can gift certificates include this treatment for far less? Could it be that they aren't giving more than a tiny amount? Once you buy that tiny amount and it doesn't work, are they selling you more and more until they finally arrive at the effective dose? Or are people just deciding BOTOX® doesn't work for them? Or are people thinking that a small, partial effect makes them look a little better, even if it has no effect at all?

Also, this medication is supposed to be stored in a refrigerated environment before it is diluted. It is then supposed to be used within about a day. After twenty-hours, it starts to lose its effects. While being stored that day, it should be correctly labeled as to its concentration and date of dilution. That way, old bottles aren't mistakenly used. Do people who work in spas do this? Does anybody receiving these shots ask these questions?

A standard of medical practice is to keep track of what you do. This way, if something doesn't work you can adjust your treatment. If something does work, you can do exactly the same thing. Are the people working in the spas keeping records of exactly what they are doing for each individual? Or are they just giving receipts? If they are keeping these records as required by law in California, that information is your property. In California, they are required to provide you with a copy if you request it. When I give BOTOX® in my office, I make a chart of where on the face each injection is given and how much each location gets. You may want to keep track of just how much of this expensive medicine you require and where it should be given.

Ptosis (Droopy Lids)

They teach us in eyeball school that the eye has to be open to see. If the eyelids droop down enough to cover the center of the eye, you can't see. Back in ancient times when I was an ophthalmology intern, my job was to sleep in the Los Angeles County Hospital and take care of all the nighttime emergencies. One night, a very concerned family brought their grandmother into the hospital because of her sudden blindness in one eye. I groggily got out of bed at 3:00 a.m. to see her. The first thing I did was to turn off all the lights. Then, in a completely dark room, I turned on the lighted eye chart and asked her to read it. When she told me she couldn't even see the eye chart, I was surprised and puzzled. This woke me up a little more. I turned on the light and looked at her. Then I noticed that the eye in question was closed! "Oh," I said, "let's try that again." I turned off the light, reached over and lifted her eyelid, and said, "Now try to read the chart."

She read all the way to the bottom! Her family and I all let out a cry of relief. She wasn't blind. And because this kind of lid-drooping wasn't an emergency, I could go back to sleep!

As the upper eyelids slowly droop more and more, the change is usually so gradual people don't notice. This grandmother had suddenly closed her open eye and then realized she couldn't see out of her eye covered by a droopy lid. The eyelid had dropped so slowly she hadn't noticed. She could see well out of the other eye. I guess she only needed one.

It is common for me to notice someone's lids cutting across half the eye in my office. When I ask them if it is causing a problem, they are usually unaware that their eyes are half closed. When I lift their eyelid and ask if they see better, they are often surprised by how much more they can see. Sometimes they admit that they hold one eye open to drive. This is okay if they have automatic transmission. But if they have to shift, they either have to take their hand off the wheel or let go of their lid and close their eyes to change gears. This is why I always recommend automatic transmission for people with droopy lids.

There are two reasons people have to hold their eyes open when they drive. First, the skin on the front of the lid tends to stretch out with age. It can become so stretchy that it hangs down over the eyelashes and blocks central vision. This skin can be removed in a way that makes the incision disappear in the natural folds of the face. When it works as planned, you look the same, except your eyes are open. When this extra skin is the only reason the lids droop, once it is removed, the eyes are wide open.

The other reason to hold your eye open while driving is that the edge of the lid droops down to cover the eye. This is not an issue of extra skin. There is a tendon that holds the eyelid up.

This tendon is attached to a muscle near the back of the eye. This muscle pulls on the tendon, which lifts the lid. If the tendon stretches enough, the lid droops down to cover the eye. An eye that is closed cannot see.

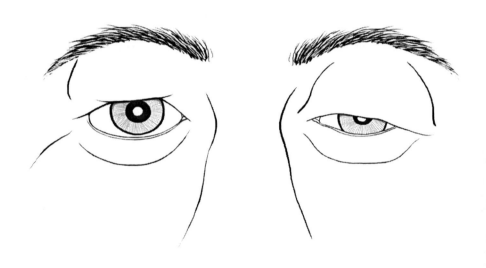

When the tendon that holds the eyelid up stretches, the edge of the lid drops. If it gets close to the center of the eye, it can reduce vision.

To fix this problem, the tendon needs to be tightened. Think of this like a rope holding the lid up. If we tie a knot in this rope, it will be shorter, and the lid will be higher. That is essentially what we do when we lift the lid. This tendon is called the levator palpebrae superioris aponeurosis. We call the surgery "levator resection." There are other ways to lift the lid, but this is the most common.

What else might be causing droopy upper eyelids? Well, there is the forehead. Of course, part of the forehead is the eyebrows. The skin of the forehead stretches out over time. That causes the brows to droop down lower than they would otherwise. If someone has extra skin on their upper lids or droopy lids, droopy brows make these other problems worse.

Usually there is a mixture of droopy lids (ptosis), droopy brows (brow ptosis), and extra skin on the upper lid (dermatochalasis). If you have all of these problems, there are two things you can easily do. One is to tilt your head back and look down your nose at everyone. The other is to use your forehead muscles to raise your eyebrows as high as you can. This looks kind of strange, but people do it.

The stretching out of these tissues is so slow that people don't notice. They simply get used to lifting their eyebrows to see. As the years go by, their lids droop more and more. They have to lift their brows higher and higher to keep their eyes open. This causes deep wrinkles on the forehead. Usually when someone raises their eyebrows as high as they can, it indicates anger or surprise.

These poor people are always coming into my office completely unaware of their angry look. They don't understand why people react to them strangely. They usually blame age. In other words, they think that many people don't like them because they are elderly. When I ask them if they are angry or surprised, they usually reply, "Of course not," and wonder why I ask.

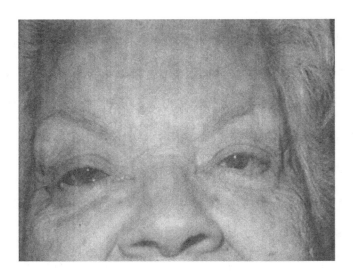

This very nice lady uses her eyebrows to lift her lids. This causes an angry or surprised look. But she is neither. She has a very pleasant personality!

When I try to get them to relax their brows to demonstrate the real position of their lids, they can't do it. I ask them to close their eyes and relax their forehead. When their forehead wrinkles relax, I ask them to open their eyes and look straight ahead without raising their brows. Sometimes they just cannot do it. Opening their eyes is so connected to raising their brows that they are not able to separate these independent movements.

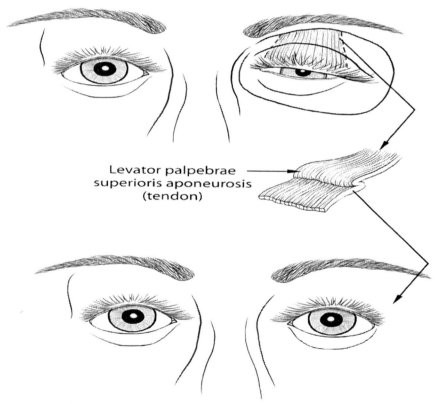

Levator palpebrae superioris aponeurosis (tendon)

To lift an eyelid, we shorten the tendon holding it up. The result is improved vision and good looks! If skin hangs down over the eyelid, it can be removed to improve vision. The scar is hidden in the natural lines of the face above the eyelashes and into the "crow's feet" wrinkles at the corner of the eye.

The constant contraction of the muscle that lifts the eyebrows can cause headaches. Late in the day, or when someone is simply tired, this muscle tends to relax. Then these people can't see. Sometimes they say that their lids only droop at the end of the day, about when they get their daily headache. Then they ask me to change their glasses to fix the problem!

The brows can be lifted many ways. The most elegant surgery is done from underneath the skin using a tiny video camera to guide the surgeon. This is called an endoscopic brow lift. The incisions are made through the scalp just above the hairline. The camera is inserted through one incision on the end of a flexible tube. Then the surgery is done through other small incisions in the scalp.

The best way to take care of droopy upper lids is to fix all three problems. They usually exist together to some degree. Ideally, we would put the eyebrows back up where they should be first. Then we would see how much the upper lids drooped from a stretchy upper lid skin (dermatochalasis) and a loose upper lid tendon (ptosis). Ideally we would then tighten the tendon that holds the upper lid at the right height (levator resection). Once we did this, the edge of the eyelids and the eyebrows would be in the right position. Then we would know exactly how much extra skin to remove from the upper lid.

Unfortunately, we almost never get to do it this way. Usually one of the three problems is the most significant. To control costs, insurance companies often will only pay for the most severe of the three problems. Also, in general these companies prefer that we do things as inexpensively as possible. Of course, this way they don't have to pay as much. We doctors don't always get to do things as perfectly as we could. This is because when we mention what the insurance company will and will not pay for, patients often say, "Just do what is covered." Because doing things this way will improve vision, we do it, even though it is only part of what we could do. This can be frustrating for those of us who find pleasure in doing a great job.

Extra skin on upper lid

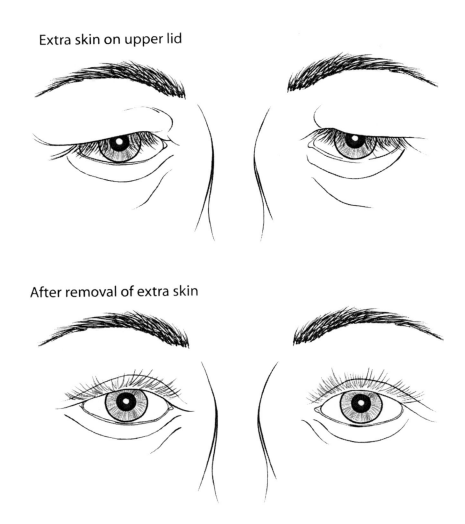

After removal of extra skin

Sometimes extra skin hangs down over the edge of the eyelid and affects vision and appearance. It can be removed so that the scars are very hard to see. They fit into the natural curves of the face.

Another form of drooping happens to the lower lids. They can droop, too! Normally the upper edge of the lower lid rests exactly at the lower border of the cornea (the clear part in the front of the eye).

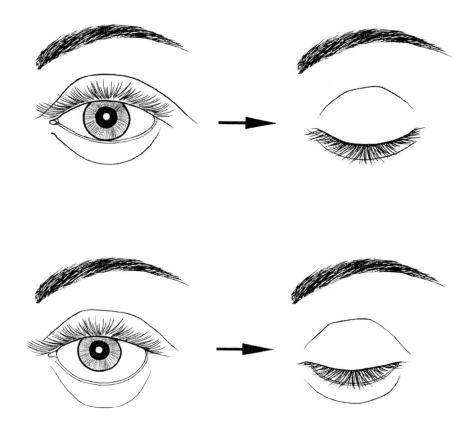

The upper figure shows the lower lid in the correct position just at the bottom edge of the colored part of the eye. This normal lid completely covers the eye when closed. The lower figure shows a droopy lower lid. When the eye blinks, the upper lid comes down to where the lower lid is supposed to be. If it is not there, the eye never closes while blinking. This causes a band of dryness across the lower eye. That can cause pain and tearing. Then, while sleeping, these eyes may not close. That causes even more pain and tearing at night and early in the morning.

The normal position of the lower lid is at the bottom of the iris (the colored part of the eye). If the lower lid droops, it falls below its normal position. Then you can see the white part of the eye (sclera) below the colored part of the eye when you look in the mirror. This could mean that your eye is staying open at night. That causes irritation and blurred vision.

When the eye closes during a blink, the upper lid comes down to where the lower lid is supposed to be. If the lower lid has drooped down below its normal position, the upper lid doesn't chase it to its lower position. Instead, the upper lid stops where the lower lid is supposed to be. Because blinking spreads moisture around the eye, if an area of the eye is uncovered, it becomes dry. This hurts, and it can be dangerous. Constant dryness of the surface of the eye can cause it to erode. If this goes far enough, a hole forms. Then the eye gets infected on the inside. This may cause permanent blindness.

Droopy lower lids may also cause the eyes to stay open while sleeping. If the eye is open all night, it dries out and really hurts when you wake up. Of course, the positive side of having your eyes open at night is that no one can sneak up on you while you are sleeping!

After you have been awake for a while, you blink a lot and spread moisture over the eye. Then it usually feels better. These people often tell me that their eyes hurt and they can't see well in the morning. When they try to read the newspaper at the breakfast table, at first they have trouble. After blinking a lot, they can see to read and their vision improves. During the day, their eyes never feel completely normal. If blinking doesn't cover the whole surface of their eyes with tears, there is always a band of dryness across the lower part of the eyes that keeps them dry and uncomfortable.

Blinking is a fascinating thing. Everyone does it a lot. The muscle that causes the eye to blink is very complex. It has three different parts. When they work together, lots of different things happen with each blink. First, there is a gland that makes most of the tears (lacrimal gland). It is under the upper lid on the outside. With each blink, the eye muscle (orbicularis oculi) pushes a little fluid out of the lacrimal gland. Then, as the lid goes down, it spreads out the tears evenly over the surface of the eye. This causes the whole front of the eye to have the same amount of moisture for a very short time. Then the eye opens again. As soon as it opens, the fluid of the tears starts to evaporate. Also, when the eye blinks, tear fluid is forced into the tear drainage system. The fluid that was forced into this system on the last blink is also forced into a collecting sac (nasolacrimal sac). The fluid that was forced into this collecting sac is then forced into the nose through a drainage tube (nasolacrimal duct).

The result of all these fluid movements is a river of tears constantly flowing across the eye. The pump is the muscle that causes the blink (orbicularis oculi). The source of the river is the gland that makes the watery part of the tears (lacrimal gland). These tears are drained through the lacrimal drainage system.

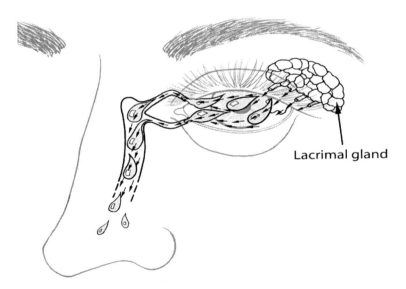

Lacrimal gland

The blink mechanism acts like a pump. It forces fluid out of the lacrimal gland onto the surface of the eye. Also, blinking forces fluid off the eye and into the tear-collecting system. Then the movement of blinking muscles forces fluid out of the tear-collecting system and into the nose.

This river of tears requires certain conditions to flow. First, it needs the eyelid to be held tightly against the eye. This way, not much fluid drops down off the eye into the area behind the lower eyelid. Instead, the fluid drops down to the top of the lower lid. This is where one of the drainage openings is. When a blink happens, this fluid is forced into both drains.

If the eyelid is turned out or droops down, the fluid doesn't flow out. Then it spills out the side of the lid. When this happens, people come to me complaining of tearing. They usually want me to change their glasses to fix the problem.

The eyelid is held in place by tendons. Inner and outer tendons hold the lid up, while the lower tendons hold the lid down. All these tendons hold the lid against the eye. When they get loose with age, the lid droops. It may also turn in or out. If it turns out, the inner part of the lid is exposed to air, causing the eye to dry out and hurt. Tears will come out in response to the pain. This is no way to live. Constant pain and tearing have to be fixed! The repair of this problem involves tightening these tendons.

Another reason for pain and tearing is when the eyelid turns in. As a result, the eyelashes rub on the eye with every blink. This really hurts. This will happen if the connections between the eye muscle that closes the lid and its structural part disconnect. If this occurs when the circular muscle that closes the eye contracts and gets smaller, it twists the skin and eyelashes inward. Thus, the eyelashes rub on the eye with every blink. Ouch! Each blink moves these lashes across the eye. This hurts! Reconnecting the two layers of the eyelid and tightening the tendons that hold the lid in place can fix this problem.

Cosmetic Eyelid and Mid-Face Surgery

I have a very prominent forehead. My eyebrows have always been low. With age, they have dropped. To open my eyes, I now have to lift my eyebrows. This causes deep wrinkles in my forehead. Of course, for a doctor, this is a good look. People interpret me as a deep thinker. I am, but the wrinkles have nothing to do with it. If my eyebrows were lifted, the wrinkles on my upper forehead would be much smaller.

Droopy upper and lower skin happen as this skin stretches out over the years. Most people think this is simply extra skin. Well, it is. However, there is another issue. The eye is sitting in a protective cushion of fat. If you get hit in the eye, it falls back on this soft cushion. So it is normal to have fat surrounding the eye. When the walls that hold this fat back behind your eyes stretch out, the fat can fall forward. Then you have bags both above and below your eyes.

To remove these bags, we usually take out both the extra skin and the fat falling forward. This is called blepharoplasty. Each person will have different amounts of fat and loose skin. Sometimes just removing the fat is enough to take away the bags. This is especially true of the lower lids. And sometimes just removing skin can work to remove bags, especially on the upper lids. Usually a mixture of skin and fat removal works best.

At this point in my discussions with patients, they may ask if just losing weight will get rid of the bags. "No," I say, "you don't have this because you are fat. This is normal fat. It isn't caused by obesity. So losing weight won't help this problem. However, that will help a lot of other things." These surgeries should be individualized. They should be discussed in detail with your surgeon.

You might ask, "If you remove this fat that protects the eye, will there be fewer cushions to protect my eyes?" The answer is yes. However, that cushion was already gone. It bulged forward and wasn't helping anything. Why does it happen? There is a "wall" that holds the fat into the socket. This is called the orbital septum. This wall stretches as you get older. The bags develop as it sags forward.

Another little-known surgery that can have a great impact on how good the face looks is the mid-face lift. As a person ages, the cheeks begin to droop. This causes something called festoons.

Fat can move forward from behind the eye to make bags below the lower lid. The cheek muscles may droop, causing a second bag called a "festoon." Both can be repaired at the same time. This can be done by removing fat, taking out extra skin, and lifting the cheek muscles.

This problem can be repaired by separating the skin and muscles of the face from the skeleton and then lifting up the whole cheek area and reattaching it to the facial bones in a higher, more normal position. To keep it high, it has to be over-lifted so that it's higher than it will be later. At first, the outer corner of the eye is higher than the middle corner. This look is temporary. The outer corner of the eye usually drops down to a natural position within two weeks. When the surgery is done successfully, a person usually looks remarkably younger. This type of facelift does not pull on the mouth at all. When I discussed this procedure with a friend and patient, he asked me, "Will I look as if my face is looking into a wind tunnel?" My answer was, "No, the triangle below your lower lid bags will disappear. Your cheeks will look higher, and you will look younger."

The bags and festoons have been removed, restoring a youthful appearance.

Rakhel Kaplan Story

By Marina Marin

Rakhel Kaplan is a good friend of Dr. May and for many years had had a few procedures done by him. "Every time a 'new thing' came along, I called her and suggested that she have it done," says Dr. May, who was also best friends with Kaplan's son in college.

Kaplan, with her interesting Israeli accent, enjoyed remembering the day she felt like she looked ten years younger. "One day we decided that it was time to have my eyelids lifted and the areas around my eyes rejuvenated. Whatever he suggests to be done, I'll do," says Kaplan, who before the surgery had droopy upper eyelids and bags under her eyes.

"I woke up from the surgery feeling groggy. I could only understand one thing he said: 'I found your cheek bones!'" This then became an inside joke which is still repeated and laughed about. During the procedure, Dr. May found Kaplan's cheekbones, once so prominent and feminine in pictures of her younger days. They had been hiding under the saggy skin around the eyes. The fleshy part of the face had fallen down off her cheek bones. When he replaced this combination of skin and facial muscles, the cheeks appeared more prominent.

"The surgery was so easy. I didn't suffer at all afterwards," she said.

Comments

Rakhel was beautiful before the surgery. She always has

been. Her inner beauty shines through, surgery or not.

Recommendations

Removing extra skin from the upper lids, lifting the upper lids, removing the bags below the eyes, lifting the cheeks, and lifting the forehead all can make people look a lot better. Lifting the eyelids and removing extra skin from the upper lids does a lot to improve vision. These are comparatively low-risk procedures that can have a big impact on people's lives.

Each person should be treated according to one's own situation and needs. Discuss these issues with your surgeon.

Chapter 12

Nutrition and the Eye

Your nutritional intake could help your vision.

About twenty years ago, it wasn't easy to find published scientific research relating nutrition and eye disease. After numerous academic studies over the years, ophthalmologists have established nutrition as a way to reduce the chance of blindness. There has been significant research about the effect of nutrition on macular degeneration. The principal focus has been on how vitamins and minerals might affect age-related eye conditions.

The Age-Related Eye Disease Study (AREDS) was a clinical trial which showed that antioxidant vitamins and zinc reduce the risk of vision loss from age-related macular degeneration (AMD). The nutrients are not a cure for AMD.

However, they may help people at high risk for developing advanced AMD keep their vision. A combination of these can be found in the supplementation formulas ICaps® or Ocuvite®. These are sold in most drug stores.

AREDS (Age-Related Eye Disease Study) Formula
How antioxidants could help your eyes.

Vitamin A (100% as beta carotene)	**75,000 IU**	**15 mg**
Vitamin C (Ascorbic acid)		**500 mg**
Vitamin E (dl-alpha tocopheryl acetate)	**400 IU**	**180 mg**
Calcium (dicalcium phosphate)		**132 mg**
Zinc (zinc oxide)		**80 mg**
Cooper (cupric oxide)		**2 mg**

An antioxidant is a chemical compound that prevents cellular damage. These chemicals are naturally present in certain foods. When talking about antioxidants, it is a good idea to understand the concept of a "free radical." A free radical is not only one of the definitions of my personality, but it is also a molecule that can damage you at the cellular level. Antioxidants prevent free radical damage and consequently protect vital molecules from harm.

One accumulates free radical damage with the passage of time, by aging. Sometimes the immune system's cells purposefully create them to combat viruses and bacteria. However, environmental pollution, radiation, cigarette smoke, herbicides, and sunlight also create free radicals. Generally, free radicals attack the nearest stable molecule, "stealing" an electron. When the "attacked" molecule loses its electron, it becomes a free radical itself, beginning a chain reaction of stealing electrons and damaging these building blocks of life (molecules). Once the process is started, it can result in the destruction of a living cell. Antioxidants are molecules which can safely interact with free radicals and terminate the chain reaction before vital tissues are damaged. They neutralize free radicals by donating one of their own electrons, ending the electron-stealing reaction.

You probably grew up hearing your parents say that carrots are good for the eyes. Well, carrots are rich in beta-carotene, which the body converts to vitamin A – a crucial nutrient for maintaining proper eyesight. So, they were right on that one. But to really lose vision from vitamin deficiency, you have to be starving. So maybe you don't really need those carrots.

The macula is a small and highly sensitive part of the retina (the film in the camera of the eye). It creates all fine-detail vision. Scientists have long known that the yellow color inside the macula comes from the carotenoids lutein and zeaxanthin (forms of vitamin A). They also believe that these plant chemicals help protect the eye by absorbing light and neutralizing free radicals. But as the body ages, the importance of carotenoids in the macula may increase because of the lifelong exposure to damaging light.

Vitamin A

Beta-carotene is a form of vitamin A. It is rich in pigments which give carrots their orange color. It is also present in many other red, yellow, and orange fruits and vegetables, as well as in dark and green leafy vegetables. You can also get it from red and purple fruits, such as cherries, grapes, and plums. The recommended dietary allowance (RDA) is 900 micrograms for men and 700 for women. Vitamin A toxicity can occur with long-term consumption of 20 milligrams or more per day.

If you are a smoker, do not take vitamin A or anything labeled as beta-carotene. Just get the amount provided by your diet. Vitamin A will increase the risk of lung cancer. The ICaps® Dietary Supplement AREDS Formula contains the same antioxidants and zinc ingredients used in the Age-Related Eye Disease Study (AREDS) without the vitamin A. It was specially designed for smokers. The trouble is, there has been no scientific study to determine if this works. However, because we don't think it will hurt and because we have nothing else, we recommend these vitamins to smokers with AMD.

When shopping for supplements, notice the various ways the dosage amounts will be written on the bottles. "% Daily Value" or "% DV" on the label is the percentage of the Daily Value, a value created by the FDA for food and supplement labeling. It's based on the RDA (Recommended Dietary Allowance). If the "% Daily Value" is 50%, then you will receive half of the FDA-recommended daily dosage of that supplement contained in one serving. Scientific units such as

"IU," "mg," and "mcg" are different ways of measuring the amounts of vitamins and minerals in each tablet. "IU" means "International Unit." It is the global standard for measuring fat-soluble vitamins and minerals such as vitamins A, D, and E. Water-soluble vitamins and supplements, such as B vitamins and vitamin C, are measured in milligrams (mg) and micrograms (mcg). One milligram (1/1000 of a gram) is equal to 1000 micrograms. Minerals that are needed in smaller amounts in the body are also measured in micrograms.

Serve fruits and vegetables raw whenever possible because vitamins can be lost from foods during preparation or storage.

Other sources of vitamin A are:

- kale
- blueberry
- broccoli
- cod liver oil
- sweet potatoes
- egg yolk
- yams
- tomato
- cantaloupe
- peaches

- bilberry or hackberry

Bilberry

You might find some vision supplementation containing the extract of the fruit bilberry. Bilberry is a cousin of the blueberry. It grows wild in the woods and forests of Europe. Some people think it promotes healthy circulation and delivers nutrients to the eyes. You also might have heard the story about the use of bilberry during World War II. Night after night during World War II, the bomber crews of Britain's Royal Air Force climbed into their planes for missions over Germany. The pilots had trouble seeing in the darkness until one man's elderly relative sent a batch of bilberry jam. Once the pilots began taking the preserves before missions, they thought they hit their targets with incredible accuracy.

And so goes the story. Truth or not, on the strength of this tale it has become one of the ten most popular herbs in the United States. It does have vitamin A and C, which are part of the AREDS formula. Since it contains these components, it may be a way to provide this combination in the diet. I know of no scientific studies on bilberry that show specific benefits to the eye.

Lutein and Zeaxanthin

Lutein and zeaxanthin are also types of vitamin A and are thought to be effective in preventing damage to the back of the eye from free radicals. Research also suggests that the intake of these two carotenoids may also provide benefits for the skin and promote cardiovascular health. They are very strongly associated with reduced risk of decreased vision from macular degeneration, if used in combination with the other supplements of the AREDS formula. There are many manufacturers of lutein. It can be found easily in the health food or drug stores.

Food sources of lutein and zeaxanthin include:

- corn
- egg yolks
- broccoli
- green beans
- green peas
- Brussels sprouts
- cabbage
- kale
- kiwi
- collard greens
- spinach

- lettuce

To maximize the absorption of these nutrients, the foods should be eaten raw or steamed lightly.

A study at the University of Southern California found that participants with the highest levels of lutein in the blood had no increase in plaque in the arteries through the 18 months of the study. Just the opposite occurred among those with the lowest lutein levels – arterial clogging worsened. The researchers also dosed sections of human arteries removed during surgery with high concentrations of lutein. They found that these arteries attracted fewer white cells, which are involved in the process that results in clogging and blockage of blood vessels.

Vitamin C

Vitamin C is an important nutrient necessary for human life. Almost all animals and plants synthesize their own vitamin C. Unfortunately, humans, apes, and guinea pigs don't. Not only are humans unable to create their own vitamin C (unlike most other species), but we also can't store it in our bodies for very long. So it is crucial to include this vitamin in the diet. It is also called ascorbic acid. This is a water-soluble vitamin present in citrus fruits and juices, including the following:

- green peppers
- cabbage
- spinach
- broccoli
- kale
- cantaloupe
- kiwi
- cilantro
- strawberries
- oranges

So how much vitamin C should you be getting? The U.S. Recommended Daily Allowance is 60 milligrams (mg) for both males and females. Intake above 2000 mg may be associated with adverse side effects in some individuals. You should absolutely get the RDA every day. If you smoke, drink, or have diabetes, you should take extra vitamin C because your levels tend to be lower than average.

Vitamin E

Vitamin E is a fat-soluble vitamin present in many foods,

especially in:

- nuts
- seeds
- vegetables
- fish oils
- whole grains (especially wheat germ)
- fortified cereals
- apricots
- sunflower seeds
- almonds
- hazelnuts

The current recommended daily allowance is 15 international units (IU) for men and 12 IU for women. Vitamin E is an antioxidant vitamin involved in the metabolism of all cells. It protects vitamin A and essential fatty acids from chemical destruction in the cells and prevents breakdown of tissues.

Eating a variety of foods that contain vitamin E is the best way to get an adequate amount. Healthy individuals who eat a balanced diet rarely need supplements. Since vitamin E is a fat-soluble vitamin, people on low-fat diets can have trouble getting enough of the vitamin.

Vitamin E deficiency can be seen in people unable to absorb fat properly. Such conditions include pancreatitis (inflammation of the pancreas), cystic fibrosis, and biliary diseases (illnesses of the gallbladder and bile ducts). Symptoms of this deficiency include muscle weakness, loss of muscle mass, abnormal eye movements, impaired vision, and unsteady gait. Eventually, kidney and liver function may be compromised.

Minerals

Your eyes can use some minerals, as well. Selenium, for example, helps your body to absorb vitamin E and helps it to make its own antioxidants. Zinc and selenium are trace minerals, which means they are needed by the human body in very small quantities.

Selenium

Selenium is a trace mineral that is essential to good health. It can be found in some meats, yeast, and seafood (like oysters). Animals that eat grains or plants that were grown in selenium-rich soil have higher levels of selenium in their muscles. In the U.S., meats and bread are common sources of dietary selenium.

Some nuts are also sources of selenium. The RDA for adults is 50 to 200 micrograms.

Zinc

Zinc is found in healthy retinal tissue. It helps your body to absorb vitamin A and is also part of an enzyme in your body that reduces the number of free radicals. Zinc has been shown to protect against macular degeneration, as part of the AREDS formula. This trace mineral is also present in a wide variety of foods. Oysters contain the highest zinc content of any food. Red meat and poultry provide the majority of zinc in the American diet. Zinc absorption is greater from a diet high in animal protein than a diet rich in plant proteins.

This trace mineral has also been associated with the male reproductive system and libido. So, the idea that oysters raise libido may be true.

Even though this mineral is an essential requirement for a healthy body, too much zinc can be harmful. More than 90 milligrams daily of zinc can be toxic. Excessive absorption can also suppress copper and iron absorption due to the antagonistic relationship of these two minerals. High levels of zinc in the AREDS study were associated with more frequent hospital admissions for urogenital disorders. However, the study also found that zinc was associated with longer life. Why? We don't know. In the future, more studies will be done about this discovery.

Other good food sources include:

- beans
- nuts
- lentils
- certain seafood
- whole grains
- fortified breakfast cereals
- dairy products

Essential Fatty Acids

Omega-3 fatty acids are considered essential to human health. The best source of omega-3 fatty acids is coldwater fish, such as salmon, mackerel, and herring. They can also be found in certain plant oils such as flaxseed oil and leafy green vegetables. Flaxseed oil has been suggested as a treatment for dry eyes (see "Dry Eyes" chapter). Extensive research indicates that omega-3 fatty acids reduce inflammation, help prevent certain chronic diseases such as heart disease and arthritis, and may reduce the risk of macular degeneration. They help to support the healthy development of eyes, skin, and joints. They may also help to maintain healthy cholesterol levels and promote good circulation, which in turn maintains a healthy heart. The heart is important because it supplies the eye with the blood it needs. Thus, it's important to maintain an appropriate balance of omega-3. These fatty acids are an FDA-approved treatment for high blood levels of certain fats (triglycerides).

Omega-3 fatty acids have three forms. The ones that actually have the beneficial effects are DHA and EPA. They are made from ALA. Some people cannot convert the ALA to DHA or EPA. There is no blood test to find out if any one person can change ALA into its active ingredients. So none of us really knows if we can convert this parent fatty acid to the effective chemical. If you take dietary supplements with high levels of ALA, you don't really know if you are getting a positive benefit.

The two sources for dietary supplements containing omega-3 fatty acids are linseed oil and fish oil. Each one has its advantages.

Sadly, the ocean and its fish are contaminated with mercury.

When we use the term fish oil, we are talking about ocean fish.

In *Alice's Adventures in Wonderland*, Lewis Carroll introduced a character called the Mad Hatter. Although Carroll's Mad Hatter was fictional, the strange and unpredictable behavior he displayed was common among people employed in the felt hat industry in the 1800s. Mercury was used in the felting process. Constant exposure to the chemical eventually caused the hatters to develop mercury poisoning. The connection between mercury poisoning and the hatters' behavior was not understood at the time, but the term "mad as a hatter" was in common usage. Mercury affects the human brain, spinal cord, kidneys, and liver. Long-term exposure to mercury can result in symptoms that get progressively worse and lead to personality changes and coma.

Fish oil may have mercury. Poisoning from mercury is a serious problem. Personally, I worry about decreased ability to think and personality changes which can be caused by this type of poisoning. That is particularly scary because it is permanent. I already have a strange personality! I don't need it to get any more bizarre. Also, I need to think as well as I can. Life is hard enough without losing this vital ability.

Linseed oil is made from plants and has high levels of

ALA. There is no mercury contamination of this source. The trouble is, I don't know if I can convert ALA to DHA and/or EPA. So, if I want to be sure I am getting the benefit of omega-3 fatty acids, I have to take fish oils.

So what do I do? Currently I am taking fish oils from small fish. "Why do you do this?" you might ask. Well, large fish like tuna or salmon live a long time. Throughout their lives, they eat little fish. If these little fish are contaminated with mercury, the amount of this toxic chemical in the big fish builds up throughout its life. The more they eat, the higher the level of mercury in the big fish.

The danger of mercury poisoning is why the current recommendations are that people eat only three servings of fish per week. That way, they get the benefit of fish oil without too much risk of mercury poisoning.

People often ask if there is any way they can get all of the omega-3 fatty acids without risk of mercury poisoning. There is. The trouble is that it is expensive. Omacor® is a purified omega-3 fatty acid pill. It is approved by the FDA for the treatment of high levels of a type of fat called triglycerides. I can write a prescription for this. It is covered under some insurance plans. The problem is that when I write this prescription, the insurance companies call me and ask, "Where's the proof that this patient has high triglycerides?" I answer that I am not prescribing it for high triglycerides. They say, "Okay, fine, we're not paying."

Recommendations

- Be familiar with the nutrition terminologies. It will help when shopping for supplements and reading about them.
- There are many ongoing studies and trials being formed constantly. Ask your doctor about supplements.
- Choose fresh squeezed juices and raw vegetables and fruits as much as possible. Your body will absorb more of the nutrients.
- If you have macular degeneration, be sure to take the recommended vitamins.

Chapter 13

Flashes and Floaters

It happens to everyone.

So the eye focuses light. The front is a lens system that focuses light onto the back of the eye. The back of the eye is like film, for it takes the light and converts it into an image that can be read by the brain. The light focused by the front of the eye has to pass through the middle of the eye to reach the part that is like film (the retina).

This middle part of the eye has to be clear for the light to pass through. This clear area in the middle of the eye is filled with a clear gel made of protein and water. My good friend and fabulous retina specialist Glen Jarus calls this the "vitreous jelly." This clear jelly is attached to the retina and other internal parts of the eye. When you are born, the gel is clear and solid like Jell-O fresh out of the refrigerator. As you get older, the center of this jelly turns mostly into liquid. Some of the gel hardens into solids. When these solids float around inside the liquid, it makes a shadow on the retina. If the background lighting is right, you can see these little things. These visible floating solid pieces of the vitreous gel are what we call "floaters."

When a person is young, only the very central part of the vitreous jelly is liquid, with solids floating around. You can tell you have floaters if, when you move your eyes, you see the particles continuing to move and then stop a second or two later. When you move your eyes, you are shaking the floaters around. When you stop, they stop. As people get older, this central liquid expands to make up a larger and larger part of the vitreous jelly. Eventually, it becomes like a water balloon. There is a very thin outer layer of solid gel. Inside this balloon are many solids floating around in a large fluid-filled cavity. Then part of this outer layer turns into liquid, and the water balloon pops. The remaining solid gel collapses into the middle of the eye. People see a sudden change in their floaters. They see this partly transparent collapsed balloon moving around inside the eye.

As the gel collapses, it pulls away from the optic nerve. The part of the gel attached to the nerve is cloudy. For complicated reasons, you don't see this clouding until the gel falls into the middle of the eye. People see the cloudy part of the gel that used to be attached to the optic nerve as a giant floater. Patients often ask me if this big floater will eventually disappear. The answer is yes and no. It will probably get smaller, but not disappear. You may just get used to it. Then they also ask me if it can be removed. The answer to this question is no. The reason is that floaters do not reduce visual function. Even a person with lots of floaters should read 20/20. Yes, these floaters are annoying and distracting. Yes, there is a surgery called vitrectomy that can remove these floaters. The trouble is that this surgery almost always causes cataracts to get worse. There is a small risk of serious complications that could result in the loss of vision and even blindness. We don't like to risk complete blindness when people function perfectly.

When the gel collapses, there is a five percent chance that a tear will form in the retina. The pulling of the gel from the back of the eye is like pulling scotch tape off paper. Sometimes the paper tears when you do this. If the retina tears, it bleeds. Blood then falls into the middle of the eye. People see this as thousands of spots floating around. Usually after the vitreous collapses, people notice they have many floaters. When a tear develops, they notice a dramatic increase in large and small dots floating through their vision.

If a retinal tear is left untreated, fluid from inside the eye goes behind the retina through the tear. Then the retina is pulled away from part of its blood supply. This causes it to stop working. If someone suddenly gets a retinal detachment, they notice a shadow or curtain coming from part of the periphery of vision. They can't see through this curtain, and it doesn't come and go. If the shadow of a retinal detachment develops, it is always there. It either gets bigger or stays the same. If a retinal detachment is left untreated, it eventually will cause blindness. This black curtain gets bigger and bigger until it swallows all the vision. It can be fixed by surgery. The earlier a retinal detachment is fixed, the better the chance for good vision.

When these people come into my office, of course I usually find nothing but a separated vitreous. In this case, I tell them to come back after two weeks to recheck for the development of a tear later. Vitreous separations may develop slowly. If they have flashes when they are away, it means the gel is pulling on the retina as it separates. If they have a sudden appearance of thousands of floaters, it means the gel tore the retina and it bled into the eye. Again, when a retinal detachment develops, people will see a shadow or a curtain coming slowly towards the middle of the eye. These things may happen after an examination by an ophthalmologist. If they do, go back!

Recommendations

Don't worry about flashes. Worry about the sudden appearance of a big floater, thousands of spots, decreased vision, or a shadow off to the side. See your ophthalmologist as soon as possible if these visual changes occur.

Chapter 14

Secrets to Good-Looking Eyes

At the beginning of my career, when I performed cosmetic surgery, my senior partner used to tease me about being a "beautician." His attitude is characteristic of most doctors. We try so hard to do a good job of diagnosing and treating medical diseases. When someone asks about appearance, it just doesn't connect with our role as physicians. I used to try to ignore these questions as distractions from the task of figuring out how to care for serious medical disease.

As the years went by, my attitude about what I should do as an ophthalmologist changed. I realized that I worked for my patients. It was my job to teach them whatever they wanted to know. Then, surprisingly, I realized that I knew the answers! Spending twenty years examining many thousands of eyes, I learned many "secrets" about appearance without even trying.

Sun Protection

Most aging is related to sun exposure. I didn't understand how true this was until I met a patient who had not been able to be in the sun for twenty years because of a medical condition. It was amazing. She was fifty and looked thirty. Her skin was smooth and unwrinkled. She had been thin all her life. That helped her not to have excess skin and added to her youthful look.

What can we learn from this fifty-year-old who looked thirty? Protect your skin from the sun as much as you can. How can you do this? Well, you could:

- Put sunscreen on every day. Reapply if you are in the sun for hours.
- Wear a hat whenever you are in the sun.
- Use sunglasses as much as possible.
- Stay out of tanning booths.
- Don't sunbathe.

All of the advice on this list will decrease exposure to sunlight. That will reduce wrinkles and changes in skin color.

Permanently Red Eyes

Another problem that seems to bother people about the look of their eyes is when they become permanently "red." Many things can cause this. Discuss why your eyes are always red with your ophthalmologist. That is the only way you can know if you have some of the very common problems discussed in this chapter.

Pingueculae and Pterygia:
Another Way the Sun Makes Your Eyes Look Bad

When I was a resident training to be an ophthalmologist, two female nursing students approached me about a problem they were having. They both noticed that they had these yellowish growths near the inner corner of their eyes. They wondered if anything serious was wrong and if anything could be done to remove them. When I asked them if they had done lots of sunbathing, these young California girls from Los Angeles said, "Of course, and we still do!" When I told them these growths were caused by sun exposure, they were suddenly silent. I could see the wheels turning in their minds, wondering if they should give up going to the beach and lying in the sun in their bikinis. After more conversation, I realized they were just going to accept this change in their appearance and keep their tanning efforts going.

If we were talking now, I would tell them to use a lot of sunscreen, do some artificial tanning, and wear sunglasses and hats to limit the sun exposure on their faces. That way they might slow the growth of these yellowish things on the white part of their eyes. These growths are called pingueculae. If they grow onto the clear part of the front of the eye, they are called pterygia. They are caused by lots of sun exposure. If they are removed surgically, they often grow back bigger and redder. We hate operating and making someone worse. These poor nursing students wanted to look good. That is part of why they spent so much time tanning at the beach. But we eye doctors do not want to make the situation even worse by removing these growths and making them grow back uglier (not to mention the loss of vision that could occur).

Reduce Inflammation

Continual irritation of the eyes and eyelids looks bad. The outer covering of the white part of the eye wraps around and covers the inside of both the upper and lower lids. Things that cause the outside of the eye to be irritated affect the inner layer of the eyelid the same way. When the inside of the eyelid is continually irritated, the outer part of the eyelid is always swollen. This causes "bags" and "puffy eyes." We ophthalmologists think of this as chronic swelling of the upper and lower lids.

There is an earlier chapter in this book titled "The Big Three." It is a discussion of three different chronic eye diseases that often happen together. One of these is a condition called blepharitis. If this disease is mixed with other common problems, the eyes are always red and the eyelids are always swollen.

If you do have blepharitis . . .
And from my perspective almost everyone does . . .

That means that normal skin germs are growing on the part of your eyelids where the lashes come out. It causes the eyes to be "red-rimmed." This means that the edges of the eyelids become irritated and red. Absolutely everyone has germs growing on their skin. These germs seem to love to grow in the warm, moist environment at the edge of the eyelid. When a lot of them grow, they cause irritation of the hair follicles that make eyelashes. These irritated hair follicles seem to make smaller, thinner eyelashes.

A conversation I often have goes like this. After the patient complains of constant eye irritation, I explain, "The edges of your lids are always red, and your lids are always swollen because you have an extra growth of normal skin bacteria at the base of your eyelashes. This is called blepharitis." My very nice elderly lady patient then says, "But doctor, I don't have eyelashes!"

It seems like this discussion happens every day in my office. These people have had normal skin germs growing at the base of their eyelashes for decades. Gradually, the follicles that make lashes are more and more damaged. They make smaller and more separated lashes. When I look at the edge of the lid with a microscope, I can see lots of thin little lashes. These people do have eyelashes. When they look in the mirror, they just can't see them.

There are special soaps designed to wash the eyelashes without irritating the eyes. This treatment is a nice place to start when people have extra growth of germs at the edge of the lid. When this treatment works, the eyes become less red. The lids are no longer swollen. That means the puffiness and bags may go away. The eyelashes are thicker and longer. Often the quality of vision improves.

The "secret" here is that washing your eyelashes with these special soaps may cause the eyelashes to become thicker and longer. These soaps can be purchased without a prescription (examples are OCuSoft® and I-Scrub®). You could try to make your lashes thicker by washing them daily. You would have to do this for at least a month before knowing if this treatment works for you.

You can make your eyelashes thicker by cutting them short.

Okay, so I admit it. This section is NOT scientific.

Right after I finished my training, I was helping my good friend and fabulous retina specialist Glen Jarus, M.D., operate on many people for their retinal detachments. This is a serious kind of eye surgery. So serious that, at the time, we cut off the eyelashes to prevent infection. Remember, the eyelashes are where germs grow.

There was a female nurse who specialized in helping Dr. Jarus in these surgeries. She noticed that when people who had already had their lashes cut short came back for another surgery, their eyelashes were thicker and longer on that side.

Then a very strange thing happened. This nice eye surgery nurse suffered a severe eye injury. She needed a series of eye surgeries. Before one of them, she called and told me to cut the lashes off both her eyes so they would grow back thicker on both sides. At that time, I was much more concerned about saving the vision. I thought she was joking or responding to the stress of her medical problem in a strange way. Totally focused on doing a good job on her surgery, I ignored her request to cut the other lashes short. Thankfully, the surgery went well. I was relieved. She called my office and left a message the next day, saying, "Don't worry about not cutting the eyelashes short on my other eye. I did it myself."

When she came back for her appointments, I realized that she was right! Her eyelashes were thicker and longer on both sides. Looking back now, I realize this is one of those secrets we serious eye doctors tend to ignore. Now that I am older and wiser, I realize that people want to see well *and* look good.

Medicines That Make Your Eyelashes Thicker and Longer

Here is another conversation I commonly have in my office. "I want to ask you to use an eye drop once a day in each eye to control your glaucoma. The trouble is, this drop could make your eyelashes thicker and longer." At this, my women patients usually start laughing. Then they say, "That is not a problem." Unfortunately, this class of eye drops for glaucoma can also cause the skin around the eye to get darker. They can make the eye permanently red.

Recently, small cosmetic companies have been putting this kind of medicine in a treatment to enlarge the eyelashes. The idea is that if you apply this medicine directly to your eyelashes, they will become thicker and longer. This may be true for some people. The trouble is, it is impossible to apply medicines only to your eye lashes. It always gets on your eyes. Then your eyes may become permanently red, and the skin around your eye may get dark. But if you have glaucoma and you are taking these drops as treatment for a medical condition, go for it! Put a lot on your lashes when you put the drop in anyway. Don't put it on more than once a day. That can make your eye pressure go up and cause permanent damage to the nerve that carries your sight. Continued nerve damage of this type can lead to permanent untreatable blindness. Usually, we think this is a bad thing.

Plucking

I often see patients who no longer have eyebrow hair. Almost all my female patients have done some plucking here. They have "sculpted" their eyebrows into a different shape. Fine! That has no impact on your health or vision. Go ahead! It doesn't matter. Remember that you are making a permanent change. If you don't want to have eyebrows, that's okay. They have no function. Complete lack of eyebrows causes absolutely no problem.

I was talking with my beautiful cousin about these issues. She told me that as part of the placement of her false eyelashes, the real lashes were pulled. Pulling eyelashes can cause permanent loss of the follicles that make them grow. I worry that my very nice cousin may be destroying her eyelashes. Then she would need false eyelashes the rest of her life. I wonder if the people in the beauty industry know this. If so, they create a permanent source of income when they cause a loss of eyelashes.

Vasoconstrictors

There are lots of over-the-counter eye drops that reduce redness. In general, they have as an active ingredient oxymetazoline or naphthazoline. These medicines make blood vessels smaller. Examples include:

Medications
• **Advanced Eye Relief Lubricant eye drops**
• **Bausch & Lomb Alaway Eye Itch relief**
• **Clear Eyes® eye drops**
• **Clear Eyes® Maximum Redness relief lubricant**
• **Murine® Eye Drops for Red Eyes**
• **On The Go Visine® Advanced Redness Relief**

Some people use them as part of a daily cosmetic routine. They work by making the blood vessels on the surface of the eye thinner. Eventually these blood vessels not only resist the shrinking effect, but they may get permanently larger. That means the eyes look red all the time. When these people come to me asking me to make these blood vessels smaller, I tell them there is nothing I can do. No medicines will shrink them. Surgery to remove them would probably cause scarring that would cause as many or more big blood vessels.

So how could you use these medicines to make your eyes look better? When you are going out or appearing in front of lots of people, go ahead. Just don't use them daily. That will backfire and cause the eyes to look permanently red.

If you cry . . .

When people cry, they often do not want anyone to know. Unfortunately, the type of tears that come out when you cry cause the lids to get swollen and the eyes to look red. So what do you do if you don't want people to know? The answer has two parts. First, put in the eye drops that get the red out. The list above includes the drops that "get the red out." Then ice your eyes to reduce the swelling. Finally, reapply your makeup.

How would this work in Los Angeles? Say you are a beautiful young actress. Your agent helped you get a great part in a movie. You put your heart into your performance. You want to prove that you are not just a pretty girl. You want the world to know you take your craft seriously and that you can act. You have been nominated for an Academy Award! Your friends all tell you that you will win. You have your acceptance speech prepared. Your parents are at the awards ceremony. But then another actress whom you hate wins! She goes on stage in front of the world to receive her award. The cameras show you crying. You use your acting ability to put on a look of admiration for this girl that you hate. Your tears seem to come from true happiness for this actress you admire so.

What do you do now? When the awards move on to another category, go to the bathroom. Take out your drops that "get the red out." Any from the above list will do. Put them in at least twice. That way, they will not get washed out by your tears. Then take out the ice bag from your purse and put it over your eyes. Call your handsome date and tell him to pull the limo to the side entrance. Then call your agent. Tell him to maintain contact with the press so you can know when they want to interview you. When the limo is ready, walk quickly to the side entrance and get in the car before paparazzi can get a picture. Once in the limo, put more ice on your eyes. Prepare yourself for your next performance, the interview on world-wide TV about your loss. When your agent calls, reapply your makeup quickly. Go on television collected, with clear eyes and un-swollen lids. Compliment the winner. Show poise. You'll get it next time.

If you want to look pretty, make sure you see well.

Meaningful looks and expressive eyes can only happen if you can see well. A nearsighted person is always tempted to look good by not wearing glasses. The problem is, when you can't see, you get this unfocused, distracted look. You don't recognize your friends. You don't return meaningful looks. You don't respond when someone smiles at you. You are detached from normal nonverbal communication and seem aloof and unreachable. You may give in to the urge to see by squinting a lot. That is not a classically attractive look. You cannot stare around in wonder. You cannot return happy looks. You don't know if someone is winking at you. Your eyes cannot "sparkle."

Changing Your Eye Color with Contact Lenses

Sometimes we do this in my office, but we tell our patients that it is a risk. Yes, you can change the color of your eyes with contact lenses. But from the point of view of someone who looks at eyes under a microscope all day long, they don't look like normal eyes. I understand that that may be all right. Having daughters, I realize that it is a female thing to want to look different from whoever you are. Fine, go ahead.

The problem with these lenses is that they can cause vision-threatening infections. Contact lenses in general can cause infections on the clear part of the eyes (the cornea). I tell my patients that when this happens, it is like a forest fire. If it goes out of control, there can be severe damage. If we catch this fire when it is small and put it out, there is almost no damage. So realize that if you are using contact lenses to change your eye color, you are taking a risk of losing your vision.

I have a patient who is a beautiful teenager. She came to me with a severe infection of the cornea. This is the clear part in the front of the eye. She saw perfectly without glasses. She got contact lenses just to change the color of her eyes. It was difficult to cure this potentially blinding infection. We did it anyway. Her infection was caused by these cosmetic lenses. She could have gone blind in that eye.

She looks great with brown eyes.

Rubbing

If your eyes are red and swollen for any reason and you rub them, they will get more red and swollen. Rubbing is a reason for your eyes to get red and swollen without anything else going on. If there are allergies or other causes of irritation, the effect is magnified. Inflamed, swollen skin seems to show wrinkles more easily. There is a medical disease that causes the eyelids to always be swollen (blepharochalasis). It shows us what the effect of rubbing irritated eyes would look like. These poor people have "bags," lots of wrinkles, and darker skin just around the eyelids. You could cause this look if you had a common reason for eye irritation and rubbed your eyes a lot. It is better to treat your itchy eyes with medicated drops to prevent itching. There are plenty of good drops for this. If your eyes are always red and your lids are always swollen, visit an ophthalmologist to find out why.

Advice

- Be sure to ask your ophthalmologist if you have dry eyes. Don't rub them if they itch. Get eye drops for this.
- If you cry, ice your eyes and put in vasoconstricting drops. Use drops "to get the red out" on special occasions. Don't use them every day.
- To look good, make sure you see well. That way you can have "sparkle" in your eyes.
- Protect yourself from the sun.
- Avoid plucking your eyelashes.

- If you want thicker, longer lashes, wash them daily with special soaps. Realize you have to do this regularly for months to see an effect.

Afterword

I hope this book has given you a deeper understanding of the eye and its diseases and treatments. While this guide is not meant to replace a visit to your ophthalmologist, it will give you the tools you need for a more productive dialogue between you and your doctor. You now have the background information to recognize common vision problems and take better care of your eyes.

I encourage you to take this book's advice to heart and remember to contact an ophthalmologist immediately if you notice any problems with your vision. It is important to seek treatment as soon as possible and take an active role in your visual health.

Printed in the United States
129297LV00001B/1-99/P

9 781432 7337